The Table
of Content

Also by Sarah Beattie

NEITHER FISH NOR FOWL:
Meat-free Eating for Pleasure

The Table of Content

A Vegetarian Dinner Party Book
for All Seasons

SARAH BEATTIE

Photographs by Patrick McLeavey

LITTLE, BROWN AND COMPANY

A *Little, Brown* Book

First published in Great Britain in 1995
by Little, Brown and Company

A CIP catalogue record for this book
is available from the British Library.

ISBN 0 316 91446 0

Typeset by Solidus (Bristol) Limited
Printed and bound in Great Britain by
BPC Hazell Books Ltd
A member of
The British Printing Company Ltd

Little, Brown and Company (UK)
Brettenham House
Lancaster Place
London WC2E 7EN

Acknowledgements

With love and grateful thanks, for support, encouragement, patience and love to:

Dylan Beattie, Magdalena Gray, Wendy Coslett, Veronica Bailey, Valerie Lowe, Jane Judd, David Willis, Maggie Blott, Roger Osborne, Janis Bright, Sue Stroud, Phil Usher, Nigel & Rolande Hinton, Andy & Pia Muir, Wolfram Altenhovel (my very own cheerleader), Peter & Vivienne Hellens, Donna & Kenny Sclater, Gill Hardacre and Class 6, Betty Dog and all other family and friends;

and Alan Samson and Andrew Gordon at Little, Brown;

particular thanks to Patrick McLeavey, Sue and Jo;

but especially to Michael Gray, who always knew when I didn't.

And, never forgetting, love to Jessamyn.

Note

Generally, each recipe serves 4–6 people.

Within each recipe you should adhere to using only one system of measurement (either metric *or* imperial), as they are not exact equivalents. Conversions also differ between recipes, and sometimes the metric equivalent in one recipe is not the same as in another. It is important not to use a conversion measurement from a recipe other than the one you are preparing, as the results may suffer!

If a recipe states 'sugar' without any qualifying description (e.g. 'caster' or 'icing'), then any sugar will suffice.

List of Illustrations

July I	Port-Poached Peaches and Dolcelatte Ice Cream
July II	Stuffed Tomatoes on Golden Salsa, with Grilled Fennel and Filled Focaccia
August I	Undey Vindaloo, with Courgette Foogath, Sag Kofta, Saffron Rice, Fresh Nectarine Chutney and Peshwari Nan
August II	Chargrilled Pizzette, with Aubergines on a Stick and Grilled Camembert and Peaches
September I	Chocolate Feuilletés with Café au Lait Cream
September II	Kiwi Clafoutis
October I	Pumpkin Risotto, with Garlic Cornsticks and Three Tomato Salsa
October II	Red Cabbage Parcels, with Carrot and Parsnip Cakes and Roast Apples
November I	Grilled Crottin with Red Onion Marmalade and Rocket
November II	Mushrooms en Chemise, with Sweet Potato Mash and Cauliflower and Broccoli
December I	Port, Stilton and Walnut Christmas Wreath, with Rosemary Roast Potatoes, Parsnip Quenelles and Brussels Sprouts with Mustard Cream
December II	Brandied Mushroom Parfait with Truffled Sauce

Introduction

Although our eating habits these days are generally less formal, the Dinner Party is alive and well. While restaurants suffered in the last recession, the Dinner Party continued unchecked. Its survival in the teeth of fast food, all day grazing, and micro-con trickery is not completely surprising.

The Dinner Party has been around for centuries, in one form or another. Ever since the seventeenth century when the medieval plan of a large central hall was abandoned for a more private dining room, the Dinner Party has become more intimate. Great plans have been hatched over them, friendships formed and many matches made, both contrived and by chance. (My own partnership started over dinner at a mutual friend's.) There is, undeniably, an element of performance, of showing off involved in Dinner Partying, but mainly it is an expression of giving and sharing. The sterility of State Banquets and Annual Dinners is in sharp contrast to the intimacy of the private Dinner Party. And restaurant meals, however grand or exclusive the venue, can not compare. The food may be better (but not necessarily), the service may be smoother (certainly not guaranteed), but there are things money cannot buy.

The Dinner Party thrives because it fulfils certain functions in a complex society in which we are largely cut off from each other. It is a time and a place where, over food, people can talk directly to each other, in close proximity. When younger, we may have shouted at each other over loud music and traded confidences on a sweaty dance floor. Now older, we may opt for quieter pleasures. In eating together, we give away many of our secrets. Marco Pierre White likens dining to making love in public. The Dinner Party is a little less public than the restaurant and therefore allows us reserved Brits to be a little more open.

The Dinner Party survives because it embraces and absorbs or eschews and ignores the food fads, fashions and trends. We can both explore the new and celebrate the traditional within an understood framework. The rituals of Dinner are familiar, they alter slightly from generation to generation, but they are essentially constant.

The best Dinner Party seems effortless. While much success hangs on the people there, food is the central focus. Although they wish to feel cherished and well cared for, guests don't want to feel responsible for a fraught host. Spontaneous feasts are fun but usually careful planning ensures your own enjoyment. Many people quail at the logistics. Balancing menus is daunting, crucial ingredients are forgotten and panic sets in after the shopping. Looking around at the bulging carrier bags, you wish Rumpelstiltskin would arrive to spin it all into gold for you before eight o'clock. Assailed by doubts, you wish you'd never invited anyone.

So how *do* you get everything ready at the right time without running yourself ragged? This book seeks to help. For every month there are two menus. Care has been taken to balance them and to make use of seasonal produce. This is not to say that imports are ignored – that would be a sad restriction on variety – but that you won't find parsnips in June or asparagus in December. This should mean that shopping is easier. For your convenience shopping lists have been prepared and a suggested action plan is given. You won't find a minute-by-minute countdown though, as everyone works at a different pace and no one should feel pressured to work to a stopwatch. The menus, lists and plans are not meant as straitjackets and can and should be varied as you see fit.

The recipes are eclectic with influences from travels (both actual and armchair) far and wide. Some are simple, some are more involved. Some are light and delicate, others are gutsy and substantial. All are arranged on the three-course format but you need not adhere to that. Short cuts and cheats are often detailed. Do not be afraid to cut corners where you will – delete a whole course or buy in a pudding or starter. It is quite acceptable in France to use *traiteurs*, one is not expected to do absolutely everything single-handedly. Here, London aside, you are thought a traitor if you resort to cook-chills from M & S. Fresh fruit – a great pile of grapes on a cake stand, perhaps – can be a fitting finale to a great meal. You need not always spend time making a lavish dessert.

Although the recipes are arranged in menus, it is anticipated that this book will also be dipped into for the occasional dish. Summery ideas can be altered to winter ones with some deft substitutions and vice versa. Starters can make lunch dishes or some main courses can be scaled down for starters. If you do not use the recipe, you may just take the idea behind it. And that is how it should be; food is such a personal thing. Be creative and experiment.

Good food can only come from good ingredients. Shop wisely. Look for the freshest and best produce. This is not necessarily the most expensive: supermarket greengrocery can be twice as pricey as farm-fresh organic vegetables. Be flexible, alter and substitute according to the market but do not compromise on quality.

There is a very wide range of ingredients in this book but there is no meat or fish. Vegetarianism has not been synonymous with hedonism and a vegetarian Dinner Party may conjure visions of beans in brown pots on scrubbed tables. A quick flick through this book will soon dispel that persistent cliché. Good food should not be pigeonholed or categorised. Whether you eat meat or not, the pleasures of *The Table of Content* are here for you.

Bon appetit,
Sarah Beattie
North Yorkshire, 1995

The Table of Content

MENUS FOR JULY

MENUS FOR AUGUST

MENUS FOR NOVEMBER

I
Grilled Crottins with Red Onion Marmalade and Rocket
Crêpes de Chine
Coconut Rice
Pickles
Almond Chocolate Marquise with Kumquats

II
La Garbure
Mushrooms en Chemise
Sweet Potato Mash
Cauliflower and Broccoli
Banana, Pecan and Maple Pudding

MENUS FOR DECEMBER

I
Guacamole Turbans
Port, Stilton and Walnut Christmas Wreath
Rosemary Roast Potatoes
Parsnip Quenelles
Brussels Sprouts with Mustard Cream
Cranberry and Orange Compôte with Brown Sugar Meringues

II
Brandied Mushroom Parfait with Truffled Sauce
Christmas en Croûte
Red Wine Sauce
Fondant Potatoes
Mixed Game Chips
Sautéed Savoy
Pastiche Gascon

Menu for January

I

Glazed Pak Choi Parcels

Topinambour and Cardamom Mousse
with Herb Butter

Roast Pumpkin

Braised Leeks

Walnut Torte with Caramelised Clementines
and Crème Chantilly

Menu for January
I

January is often gloomy, spirits are low after the pleasures of the festivities. The combination of flavours in this menu is designed to perk up the jaded.

You can prepare and cook everything in 2 hours but if you need to get ahead, the parcels can be made the night before and left covered in the fridge. You can make the torte the previous day – leave it in the tin and before serving warm it through in a moderate oven and then turn out.

SHOPPING LIST

Greengrocery
about 1 kg/2 lb large-leaved pak choi or Swiss chard
250 g/8 oz carrots
125 g/4 oz shiitake mushrooms
1 medium sweet red pepper
1 large onion
60 g/2 oz beansprouts
2.5 cm/1 in peeled fresh ginger
spring greens to make Chinese seaweed – optional
1.5 kg/3 lb pumpkin
750 g/1½ lb slender leeks
500 g/1 lb topinambours (Jerusalem artichokes)
1 large bulb of garlic
chervil
thyme
3 clementines
1 orange

Dairy
150 ml/5 fl oz double cream
150 ml/5 fl oz milk
150 ml/5 fl oz Greek yoghurt *or* whipping cream
340 g/12 oz butter
5 eggs

Grocery
150 g/5 oz shelled walnuts
light muscovado sugar
plain flour
baking powder
rapeseed or corn oil
½ bottle Muscat de Frontignan
cardamom pods
bread
shoyu soy sauce
runny honey
30 g/1 oz tamarind paste
sesame oil
cornflour
300 g/12 oz rice noodles

SUGGESTED ACTION PLAN

1 Make walnut torte and put in the oven.
2 Make parcels.
3 Peel and cook artichokes.
4 Do pumpkin and leeks.
5 Make mousse.
6 Do the glaze.
7 Steam the parcels, soak the noodles.
8 Whip the cream.
9 Chop the herbs, melt the butter.
10 Serve.

Glazed Pak Choi Parcels

about 1 kg/2 lb large-leaved pak choi – if unavailable use Swiss chard
– allow 3 or 5 leaves per person depending on size
250 g/8 oz carrots
125 g/4 oz shiitake mushrooms
1 medium sweet red pepper
1 large onion
60 g/2 oz beansprouts
2 cloves garlic
2.5 cm/1 in peeled fresh ginger
2 tsp cornflour
4 tbs shoyu soy sauce
2 tbs runny honey
30 g/1 oz tamarind paste
sesame oil
300 g/12 oz rice noodles
spring greens to make Chinese crispy seaweed – optional
300 ml/½ pt boiling water

Cut the carrot, mushrooms, red pepper and onions into small matchsticks. Crush the garlic. Heat a tablespoon of the sesame oil in the bottom of a wok and fry the garlic in it briefly. Grate the ginger and add half to the wok. Cook for 30 seconds then add the prepared vegetables. Stir-fry until almost tender then add the beansprouts. Slake the cornflour with 1 tbs of soy sauce and 1 tbs water. Pour over the vegetables and stir around over the heat just 1 minute longer.

Clean the pak choi leaves and blanch in boiling water. Drain and lay out on a clean tea towel. Remove any hard stem. Place 1–2 teaspoons of the filling mixture at the base of the leaf. Fold in the sides and roll up. Place the parcels in a steamer to reheat when necessary.

Pour 300 ml/½ pt of boiling water onto the tamarind paste. Leave to stand for 20 minutes. Gently fry the remaining ginger in 1 tbs of sesame oil. Add the remaining soy sauce and the honey.

Strain the tamarind water into the pan, rubbing any pulp through but discarding the seeds and fibres. Boil hard until reduced by half. Keep warm.

Plunge the rice noodles into boiling water. Allow to return to boil, stir, switch off heat and keep covered. Stand five minutes. Drain and place a neat round of noodles on each plate. Top with the reheated parcels and spoon over the glaze.

Serve immediately with an optional garnish of deep-fried fine shredded greens (Chinese crispy seaweed) or carrot 'flowers'. The flowers are formed by cutting 5 or 7 V-shaped channels the length of the carrot. Slicing the carrot crosswise, you end up with pretty 5- or 7-petalled flowers.

Topinambour and Cardamom Mousse
with Herb Butter

500g/1lb topinambours (Jerusalem artichokes)
breadcrumbs
4–5 cardamom
150ml/5fl oz milk
2 egg whites
150ml/5fl oz double cream
4 egg yolks
150g/5oz butter
3 tbs finely chopped chervil (reserve tiny sprigs for garnish)
salt
pepper

Butter six oval ramekins. Cover the bases and sides with breadcrumbs. Peel the topinambours and cook in boiling water until soft – about 15–20 minutes. Split the cardamom pods and scrape out the seeds. Crush them then add to the milk. Heat gently and infuse whilst the topinambours are cooking. Drain the topinambours and mash well. Strain the milk into the purée and, stirring well over a low heat, cook for 3 minutes. Season with salt and, if liked, a little white pepper.

Whisk the egg whites until stiff then, in a separate bowl, whip the cream until stiff – in this order you can use the same whisk. Beat the yolks into the purée then fold through the cream and egg whites. Spoon into the prepared dishes and stand in a roasting tin of hot water. Bake at 180°C/350°F/gas mark 4 for 35–40 minutes until set. Allow to stand for five minutes, before turning out. Run a round-bladed knife around the edge before inverting onto a plate. Pour around the herb butter and place a tiny sprig of chervil on top of each mousse.

Herb butter: simply melt the butter slowly in a small pan with the chopped herbs and season well with salt and pepper. Do not allow to brown.

Roast Pumpkin

a 1.5 kg/3 lb pumpkin
rapeseed or corn oil
salt

Cut the pumpkin in quarters and scrape out the seeds and fibrous, stringy parts. Reserve a handful of seeds. Peel the pumpkin and cut into chunks. Heat a 0.75 cm/¼ in film of oil in a thick roasting tin. Turn the pumpkin in the hot oil and place in the oven until nicely browned – about 30 minutes at 220°C/425°F/gas mark 7. Baste occasionally. Wash the seeds, removing any fibres. Dry and then cook under a medium grill or in an ungreased frying pan. Toast until a pale biscuity colour, shaking the pan frequently. Sprinkle generously with salt. Scatter over the top of the roast pumpkin when serving.

Braised Leeks

750 g/1½ lb slender leeks
5 cloves of garlic
30 g/1 oz butter
200 ml/7 fl oz Muscat de Frontignan
thyme
salt
pepper

Wash the leeks and trim. Cut into 5 cm/2 in lengths. Peel and slice the garlic. Melt the butter in a heavy-bottomed pan. Add the leeks and garlic. Cook slowly for ten minutes, with the lid on, shaking the pan occasionally. Add the wine, chopped herbs, salt and pepper. Simmer, covered, until the leeks are meltingly tender. Reduce the liquor by turning up the heat. Serve hot.

Walnut Torte with Caramelised Clementines and Crème Chantilly

Torte
150g/5oz shelled walnuts
150g/5oz plain flour
½ tsp baking powder
175g/6oz light muscovado sugar
3 clementines
150g/5oz butter, softened
1 egg
150ml/5fl oz Greek yoghurt or

Crème Chantilly
2 tbs honey
1 tsp finely grated orange rind
1 tsp orange juice
150ml/5fl oz whipping cream

Finely grate the walnuts. Sieve together the flour and baking powder. Well grease a 22cm/8½in cake tin. Line the base with silicone paper and grease it very well. Shake 25g/1oz of the sugar over the base. If your clementines have nice thin skins, do not peel but scrub well in hot water. Otherwise peel. Cut in half transversely.

Beat the butter, remaining sugar, flour, egg and walnuts together very well. Place the cake tin in a 180°C/350°F/gas mark 4 oven until the sugar melts then put the clementines around the base of the tin, cutside down. Cover with the walnut mixture, levelling the top. Bake for about 45–50 minutes. When firm and lightly browned, leave to cool, in the tin, for 1 hour. Invert onto a plate and carefully peel back the paper. Serve wedges just warm with Crème Chantilly or Greek yoghurt.

Crème Chantilly: warm the honey with the orange rind and 1 tsp juice, just enough to make it runny. Cool. Whip 150ml/5fl oz whipping cream. As it begins to stiffen, whisk in the honey.

Menu for January

II

MARINATED FETA ON MÂCHE WITH SESAME CROÛTONS

MUSHROOMS BOURGUIGNONNE
SALSIFY AND CARROTS
RUBY CHARD
ROAST POTATOES

STEAMED VERMICELLI PUDDINGS
WITH MARMALADE SAUCE

Menu for January
II

The Greek-influenced salad, with its clear, uncomplicated flavours, is a great start for a winter meal. 'Growing herbs' are now widely available and even if their flavours are not as pungent as those grown in the Mediterranean they do lend a touch of sunshine to our dismal winter.

The robust gutsiness of the main course contrasts well with the starter. If you cannot find salsify, use cubes of celeriac or parsnips instead.

The puddings are adapted from Victorian recipes. Home-made marmalade will give you the best results but if you haven't made use of the recently arrived Seville oranges, buy a really good jar – cheaper ones don't have enough oomph.

SHOPPING LIST

Greengrocery
2 bunches/bags of mâche (lambs' lettuce), *or* 1 bunch mâche and 1 Little Gem lettuce
450g/1lb shallots or pickling onions
1 bulb garlic
450g/1lb carrots
450g/1lb salsify
3 unwaxed lemons or 1 lime and 2 lemons
700g/1½lb ruby chard
6 large King Edward potatoes
1kg/2lb mixed mushrooms – flats, chestnut or shiitake
celery
1 bay leaf
fresh or dried thyme
mint
2 bunches flat-leaved parsley

Dairy
8 eggs
250g/8oz unsalted butter
125g/4oz Passin or Gruyère cheese
200g/6oz feta
568ml/1pt milk

Grocery

pink peppercorns
white peppercorns
black peppercorns
coarse sea salt
sugar
extra virgin olive oil
sunflower oil
white bread
white sesame seeds

½ bottle of Burgundy
plain flour
smooth Dijon mustard
dried vermicelli
marmalade
60g/2oz dried wild mushrooms – optional
25g/1oz raisins – optional
whisky – optional

SUGGESTED ACTION PLAN

1 Prepare feta and leave to marinate.
2 Make croûtons.
3 Cook mushrooms and whilst they are simmering prepare choux paste.
4 Soak vermicelli.
5 Do potatoes. Whilst they are parboiling, prepare salsify and carrots.
6 Make puddings.
7 Prepare marmalade sauce.
8 Put the choux on the mushrooms.
9 Prepare the chard – but cook only when dishing up the main course.
10 Assemble salad and serve.

Marinated Feta on Mâche with Sesame Croûtons

200g/6oz feta
a small bunch of fresh or dried thyme
a few sprigs of mint
a small bunch of flat parsley
a few pink peppercorns
a few white peppercorns
a few black peppercorns
a good pinch of coarse sea salt
a pinch of sugar
1 unwaxed lemon
3 tbs best extra virgin olive oil
6 slices of white bread
butter
1 egg white
2 tsp white sesame seeds
2 bunches/bags of mâche (lambs' lettuce), or 1 bunch mâche and
1 Little Gem lettuce

Cut the feta into small cubes and place in a shallow bowl. Chop the herbs finely. Grind the peppercorns, salt and sugar together, fairly coarsely. Grate the zest from the lemon, either with a zester to make tiny streamers or on a fine grater. Combine the herbs, rind and peppercorns and sprinkle over the feta. Squeeze the lemon juice over and then drizzle on the olive oil. Turn about carefully so all the feta is coated then leave in a cool place for at least 1 hour.

Trim the bread into neat shapes, removing the crust – they can be square, round, hexagonal or whatever. Butter a thick baking tray. Lightly whisk the egg white and dip the bread into it. Spread the sesame seeds on a plate and coat both sides of the bread with them. Place on the baking sheet and put in a hot oven 220°C/425°F/gas mark 7 until crisp and nicely browned, about 10 minutes.

Divide the washed mâche (and lettuce if using) between the plates, arranging it nicely. Top with a croûton and then pile on the feta cubes. Dribble over any remaining marinade and serve.

Mushrooms Bourguignonne

450g/1 lb shallots or pickling onions
4 cloves garlic
30g/1 oz butter
a few peppercorns
1 kg/2 lb mixed mushrooms – use big flat open ones, chestnut or shiitake
3 celery leaves
a bunch of flat-leaved parsley
60g/2 oz dried wild mushrooms – optional
a bay leaf
½ bottle of Burgundy

Choux
250ml/9 fl oz water
100 g/3½ oz butter
150g/6 oz plain flour
4 eggs lightly beaten
1 tsp smooth Dijon mustard
125g/4 oz Passin or Gruyère cheese

Peel and trim the shallots or onions. Quarter if large but otherwise leave whole. Roughly chop the garlic. Set both to brown gently in a deep heatproof casserole in the butter. Crack the peppercorns and sprinkle them over the shallots. Clean the mushrooms and cut into large chunks. Add to the pan.

Roughly chop the celery leaves and parsley (including the stalks). Grind the dried mushrooms finely. Add to the pan with the bay leaf and the wine. Season well. Cover and simmer for 30 minutes either on top of the stove or in the oven.

To make the choux, melt the butter in the water. Tip in the flour and beat hard over a low heat until the mixture forms a ball and leaves the sides cleanly. Take off the heat and add the eggs a little at a time, beating well. Beat in the Dijon mustard. Dice the cheese and combine with the paste. Season with a little salt and pepper. Leave until cold.

Thirty minutes before serving, using two wetted spoons carefully drop egg-sized ovals of paste around the edge of the hot mushroom mixture. Place in a very hot oven 220°C/425°F/gas mark 7 until puffed and golden. Serve immediately.

Salsify and Carrots

450 g/1 lb carrots
450 g/1 lb salsify
butter
a lime or lemon
pepper
salt

Choose carrots and salsify of a similar thickness. Scrape or peel and cut into 5 cm/2 in lengths. Thickly butter a lidded baking dish and lay the carrot and salsify pieces, alternating, neatly side by side. Squeeze over the lime or lemon juice. Dust with salt and pepper. Cover tightly and bake for 1 hour in a moderate oven until tender. The temperature is not crucial – in a little hotter oven, reduce the time allowed.

Ruby Chard

700 g/1½ lb ruby chard
a little oil

Wash the chard and trim the stems. Pull the brightly coloured stems away from the leaves. Cut into 1 cm/½ in pieces. Shred the leaves. Heat the oil in a large pan. Fry the stem pieces for a minute, shaking or stirring to avoid sticking. Add the shredded leaves and cook a bare minute longer. Serve.

Roast Potatoes

6 large King Edward potatoes
sunflower oil

Wash the potatoes and place them whole into a large pan of boiling salted water. Cook 10 minutes. Drain, cool slightly then peel. Cut each potato into four – quartering them lengthwise. Pour sunflower oil into a roasting tin to a depth of 0.5 cm/¼ in. Heat it in a hot oven 220°C/425°F/gas mark 7, then turn the potatoes in the hot oil. Roast until crisp and deep golden brown, about 30 minutes.

Steamed Vermicelli Puddings with Marmalade Sauce

75 g/3 oz dried vermicelli, broken up
568 ml/1 pt milk
3 eggs
50 g/2 oz sugar
3 tbs marmalade
25 g/1 oz raisins – optional
unsalted butter
1 lemon
whisky – optional

Heat the milk and, when scalding, pour over the vermicelli. Allow to stand 20 minutes. Grease 6 individual pudding basins or ramekins. Beat together the eggs, sugar and 1 tbs of marmalade. Beat in the vermicelli, milk and raisins. Divide between the basins. Cover with buttered papers and steam until firm, about 25–30 minutes, *or* stand in a roasting tin of boiling water and bake at 180°C/350°F/gas mark 4 for 30–35 minutes.

The puddings can be inverted onto serving plates by running a round-bladed knife around the edges to loosen first.

Combine the remaining marmalade in a small pan with the juice of the lemon, a knob of butter, 4 tbs water and whisky and sugar to taste. Boil a few minutes. Strain if a clear sauce is desired.

Menu for February

I

Hot Sour Soup

Celeriac Feuilleté
Stir-Fried Red Cabbage with Walnuts
Sherried Shiitake Sauce

Apple Coeur à la Crème

Menu for February

I

The head-clearing starter is Thai-based. It is very warming and gives a comforting glow.

Celeriac shows off its versatility in the main course, being both smooth and creamy and crisp and crunchy. Red cabbage is thought of in terms of long slow braising but in this recipe it is cooked at the last minute. Aside from the pudding, which must be made well ahead, the rest of the meal can be completed in an hour.

SHOPPING LIST

Greengrocery
4 red onions
2 shallots
1 bulb garlic
2 baby leeks
125 g/4 oz shiitake mushrooms
125 g/4 oz oyster mushrooms
1 small kohlrabi
1 carrot
1 lime
1 large + 1 small celeriac
1 red cabbage
coconut – see GROCERY
pineapple
3 large Granny Smith apples
4 blood (ruby) oranges
2 green chillies
fresh root ginger

fresh coriander
Kaffir lime leaves
lemon grass
1 pomegranate – optional

Dairy
225 g/8 oz Ricotta
225 g/8 oz Mascarpone
225 g/8 oz strained Greek yoghurt
50 g/2 oz butter

Grocery
1 lt/1¾ pt vegetable stock
shoyu soy sauce
150 ml/5 fl oz coconut milk (fresh or tinned)
allspice berries
star anise
nutmeg
sunflower oil
sesame oil
125 g/4 oz shelled walnuts
plain flour
½ bottle dry sherry
a small jar runny honey

SUGGESTED ACTION PLAN

1 Make pudding.
2 Prepare soup up to the addition of the coconut.
3 Cook the celeriac purée and cut the slices.
4 Prepare the cabbage.
5 Make the sauce.
6 Fry celeriac slices/cook cabbage.
7 Finish the soup and serve.

Hot Sour Soup

2.5 cm/1 in piece of fresh root ginger
2 tbs sesame oil
2 red onions
4 cloves garlic
2 baby leeks
125 g/4 oz oyster mushrooms
1 small kohlrabi
1 carrot
2 green chillies
1 lt/1¾ pt vegetable stock
2 tbs shoyu soy sauce
2 slices fresh pineapple
a few stalks of coriander
4 Kaffir lime leaves
1 stalk lemon grass
150 ml/5 fl oz coconut milk (fresh or tinned)
1 lime
1 pomegranate – optional

Finely grate the ginger and combine it over a low heat with the sesame oil. Shred all the vegetables into fine strips. Deseed and slice the chillies. Place the vegetables and chillies in the gingered oil and cook, stirring, over a relatively high heat for 3 minutes. Add the stock and shoyu.

Cut the pineapple into small cubes and add to the soup with the chopped coriander and crumbled lime leaves. Bash the lemon grass with a rolling pin and add it to the soup. Simmer for 10 minutes, then stir in the coconut milk. Taste and if necessary sharpen with a little lime juice.

Reheat gently before serving. You can garnish with a Kaffir lime leaf topped with a few pomegranate seeds if desired.

Celeriac Feuilleté

1 large + 1 small celeriac
2 cloves garlic
2 star anise
25 g/1 oz butter
nutmeg
black pepper
sunflower oil
salt

Peel and cube the large celeriac. Cook it in a large pan of boiling water to which you have added 2 peeled cloves of garlic and two whole star anise. Simmer until tender.

Meanwhile, peel the other celeriac and slice into thin rounds. Heat some oil for deep frying. Drain the cooked celeriac reserving the cooking water. Remove the star anise. Mash very well then beat in the butter, freshly grated nutmeg and freshly ground black pepper. Add as much of the cooking liquid as necessary to make the purée the consistency of whipped cream. Keep hot.

Deep fry the celeriac slices until crisp and brown. Drain well on kitchen paper and sprinkle with salt. Layer up with the purée and serve immediately.

Stir-Fried Red Cabbage with Walnuts

1 red cabbage
2 red onions
2 cloves garlic
4 allspice berries
125 g/4 oz shelled walnuts
sunflower oil

Finely shred the cabbage and onions. Crush the garlic. Grind the allspice berries and place in a large pan over a moderate heat. Shake the pan and cook for half a minute before adding the roughly chopped or broken walnuts. Dry fry for a minute or two then remove from the heat and place on a plate to cool. Pour a little oil into the pan and cook the vegetables quickly until they are just softened. Stir in the walnut/allspice mixture. Serve.

Sherried Shiitake Sauce

2 shallots
2 cloves of garlic
25 g/1 oz butter
sugar
125 g/4 oz shiitake mushrooms
1 tbs plain flour
200 ml/7 fl oz dry sherry
salt
pepper

Finely chop the shallots and garlic. Fry gently in the butter until soft. Add a pinch of sugar and turn up the heat to caramelise slightly. Quarter the mushrooms and fry with the shallots for 2 minutes. Sprinkle over the flour and stir over a moderate heat until the flour is lightly browned. Slowly stir in the sherry and simmer for 5 minutes, stirring occasionally. Season well.

Apple Coeur à la Crème

3 large Granny Smith apples
4 blood (ruby) oranges
225 g/8 oz Ricotta
225 g/8 oz Mascarpone
225 g/8 oz strained Greek yoghurt
runny honey

Coeur à la crème should be made in pierced china heart-shaped moulds, but if you don't have any drain the cream mixture first in a cheesecloth-lined sieve for a few hours before filling small moulds or ramekins.

Cut the apples into quarters and remove the cores. Slice thinly into an enamel or stainless steel pan. Finely grate the orange zest and leave to one side. Squeeze the oranges over the apple slices and then simmer gently until the apples have coloured. Allow to cool completely.

Beat together the Ricotta, Mascarpone and yoghurt. Beat in the orange rind and honey to taste, about 3 or 4 tablespoons. Line six moulds with cheesecloth or *in extremis* cling film. Neatly place a layer of overlapping apple slices in the base of each mould. Reserve the cooking juice. Fill each mould with the cream cheese mixture, packing down well and levelling the tops. Refrigerate for at least 3 hours.

Add more honey to the orange cooking liquor, warming slightly to make a syrup. Allow to cool.

To serve: turn each mould out onto a separate plate and carefully peel back the cheesecloth. Drizzle over the orange syrup and decorate with a couple of early violets or primroses if available.

Menu for February

II

BLINIS AND SMOKED AUBERGINE

RED ONION FLAMICHE – A VALENTINE'S TARTE
POTATOES ANNA GAURIN
BROCCOLI

CHAMPAGNE SNOW AND LYCHEES

Menu for February
II

Unusual flavours perfume this unashamedly romantic menu. Both Mardi Gras and Valentine's Day are celebrated with Russian pancakes and hearts and flowers.

Save time on the day by smoking the aubergine and making the snow the night before.

Cheaper sparkling wines can be used for the snow – add a little Crème de Cassis for colour if liked. (A Kir snow, maybe?)

Try to find fresh lychees, they should be at their best, plump and scented. Peel them over the sundae glasses to catch that fragrant juice.

SHOPPING LIST

Greengrocery
1 large aubergine
1 large Bramley apple
1 small beetroot
2 large red onions
1 bulb garlic
a sprig of rosemary
900 g/2 lb medium-sized potatoes – use Desirée or King Edward's
parsley
700 g/1½ lb broccoli
2 lemons
18 lychees

Dairy
8 eggs

568 ml/1 pt milk
290 g/9½ oz butter
150 ml/5 fl oz smetana (soured cream)
350 g/12 oz cottage cheese
150 ml/5 fl oz crème fraîche

Grocery
lapsang souchong tea
buckwheat flour
plain flour
instant dried yeast
oil
sesame oil
blue poppyseeds
black onion seeds
nutmeg
white pepper
icing sugar
granulated sugar
caster sugar
¼ bottle red wine
bottle (pink) champagne
crystallised rose petals – optional

SUGGESTED ACTION PLAN

1   Make snow.
2   Smoke aubergine, cook garlic.
3   Make batter.
4   Make pastry.
5   Do apple and beetroot, dry fry seeds.
6   Make flamiche.
7   Do potatoes, prepare onions, broccoli and lychees.
8   Cook blinis and serve.
9   Grill flamiche top, cook broccoli.

Blinis and Smoked Aubergine

1 large aubergine
50g/2oz lapsang souchong tea
125g/4oz buckwheat flour
125g/4oz plain flour
6g/¼oz instant dried yeast
pinch salt
300ml/½pt scalded milk
2 eggs
40g/1½oz melted butter
oil or butter
1 large Bramley apple
1 small beetroot
1 tsp blue poppyseeds
½tsp black onion seeds
150ml/¼pt smetana (soured cream)

Thinly slice the aubergine. Place the tea in a roasting tin. Cover it with a rack. Lay the aubergine slices on the rack and cover the whole with foil. Bake for 30 minutes at 200°C/400°F/gas mark 6.

Meanwhile make the batter. Sift the flours, yeast and salt into a big bowl. Make a well in the centre and pour in the cooled but still warm milk. Draw the flour in to the liquid gradually. Beat well to make a smooth batter. Cover the bowl with a clean tea towel and leave in a warm place for thirty minutes until doubled in bulk and bubbly.

Whilst the batter is proving, peel and core the apple. Place in a small covered pan and cook with a tablespoon of water until the flesh has disintegrated into a soft mass. Wash the beetroot and finely grate it. Combine with the apple. Leave to chill. Dry fry the seeds in a small pan.

Lightly beat together the egg yolks and melted butter. Knock back the batter with a spoon and then whisk in the egg/butter mixture. Whip the egg whites until stiffly peaking and fold through the batter.

Heat a large heavy-based frying pan or griddle, grease with a little melted butter. Spoon ladlefuls of batter onto the hot pan. When the top has 'set' and the bottom is golden, lay an aubergine slice on the top of each blini then flip over and cook the aubergine side until golden. Keep warm whilst cooking the rest.

To serve: place 2 or 3 blinis on each plate with a spoon of the apple/beetroot mixture and a dollop of smetana crowned with a sprinkle of toasted seeds.

Red Onion Flamiche – A Valentine's Tarte

250g/8oz plain flour
a good pinch of salt
125g/4oz soft butter or vegetable margarine
3 egg yolks
50ml/2fl oz milk
3 eggs
350g/12oz cottage cheese
150ml/5fl oz crème fraîche
nutmeg
white pepper
2 large red onions
sesame oil
icing sugar

Sift the flour with the salt. Make a well in the centre. Cut the butter into small pieces. Place in the well with the egg yolks and milk. Mix well with the fingertips drawing in the flour. Knead lightly then roll out to line a large heart tin or 25cm/10in flan ring or dish. Chill well.

Put the eggs, cottage cheese and crème fraîche in a liquidiser or food processor and run until smooth. Season well with plenty of nutmeg and white pepper.

Pour the mixture into the pastry shell and bake at 220°C/425°F/gas mark 7 until firm.

Peel and slice the red onions thinly. Spread over the tart. Dribble over the sesame oil and dust liberally with icing sugar. Caramelise under a hot grill and serve.

Potatoes Anna Gaurin

150ml/5fl oz red wine
1 bulb garlic
a sprig of rosemary
900g/2lb medium-sized potatoes – use Desirée or King Edward's
125g/4oz butter
salt
pepper
parsley

Put the wine, garlic and rosemary in a small covered casserole and simmer (either on the hob or in the oven) until the garlic is very soft. Rub through a sieve, do not liquidise.

Peel the potatoes and cut into neat cylinder shapes – use the trimmings for soup or stews. Slice the cylinders into thin rounds. Wash then dry the slices on a clean towel. Don't be tempted to miss this stage out – it matters. Dust with salt and pepper.

Melt the butter in a heavy frying pan. Sauté the potatoes in the butter making sure that all the slices are well coated. Press into a big cake and fry until the bottom is golden. Invert the potato cake onto a baking tray then slide it back into the pan to cook the other side. Spread the top with the garlic paste and sprinkle thickly with chopped parsley.

Broccoli

700g/1½lb broccoli
1 lemon

Wash the broccoli. Break it up into little florets and slice the thick stalks thinly. Either steam or boil in a minimum of water until just tender. Squeeze over some lemon juice and serve immediately. With the buttery richness of the potatoes and the tart it is necessary to serve a very simple green vegetable.

Champagne Snow and Lychees

150ml/5fl oz water
150g/5oz granulated sugar
1 lemon
1 × 70cl bottle champagne (if you can find pink so much the better)
3 egg whites
150g/5oz caster sugar
18 lychees
crystallised rose petals – optional

Dissolve the granulated sugar in the water and bring to the boil. Cool. Squeeze the lemon and strain the juice into the syrup. Add the champagne. Pour into a large flat dish and freeze until going mushy around the edge. Lightly whip one of the egg whites until just frothy then beat into the champagne mixture. Return to the freezer.

Whisk the remaining egg whites until softly peaking. Whisk in half the caster sugar a little at a time then fold in the remainder. Fold into the still sloppy semifrozen champagne mixture. Mix carefully then freeze until firm. Cover tightly.

To serve: allow the snow to soften 20 minutes in the fridge before scooping into sundae glasses. Add three peeled lychees to each glass and sprinkle with rose petals if desired.

Menu for March

I

Watercress Soup and Mustard Sablé Crackers

Layered Polenta wrapped in Chard
Grilled Endive and Orange Butter
Deep-Fried Onion Rings

Rhubarb and Ginger Tiramisù

Menu for March
I

$\mathcal{S}$ ome of this menu needs to be made in advance (the polenta, the tiramisù) but most of it can be prepared the night before with only the last minute cooking of the endive and onion rings. The soup is best 'finished' on the day but the stock can be made at least 2 days in advance. The sablé crackers will keep in an airtight tin for a day or so.

Tadcaster in North Yorkshire is famed not only for the large brewery but also for its fine forced rhubarb. It is essential that the rhubarb used is very slender – if outdoor rhubarb is all that is available, check out the Sonagold plums or Moroccan strawberries that are around.

SHOPPING LIST

Greengrocery
4 large onions
1 bulb garlic
2 large carrots
4 sticks celery
125 g/4 oz mushrooms
2 bunches watercress
2 shallots
450 g/1 lb approx chard or spinach leaves
9 chicons of chicory
2 sweet oranges
450 g/1 lb pink, fine rhubarb
a bay leaf
a good sprig of thyme

Dairy
155 g/6 oz butter
9 eggs
50 g/2 oz unsalted butter
50 g/2 oz Parmesan
450 g/1 lb Mascarpone

Grocery
wheatmeal flour
plain flour
dry mustard
wholegrain mustard
celery salt
peppercorns
nutmeg
ground ginger
1 knobble stem ginger
honey
oil
450 g/1 lb fine yellow polenta (cornmeal)
400 g/14 oz tin of plum tomatoes in juice
caster sugar
golden caster sugar
sunflower oil
½ bottle ginger wine – not the 'green' variety

SUGGESTED ACTION PLAN

1   Make polenta, stock, crackers and tiramisù the day before.
2   Bake polenta.
3   Finish soup.
4   Make onion rings and grill endive.

Watercress Soup
and Mustard Sablé Crackers

Crackers
125 g/5 oz wheatmeal flour
a good pinch dry mustard
1 tbs sugar
½ tsp celery salt
75 g/3 oz butter
2 egg yolks
1 tsp wholegrain mustard
1 tbs honey

Stock
2 large onions
2 cloves garlic
2 large carrots
4 sticks celery
a little oil
1.25 lt/2 pt water
125 g/4 oz mushrooms
a few peppercorns
a bay leaf
a good sprig of thyme

2 bunches watercress
2 shallots
2 cloves garlic
30 g/1 oz butter

Sift together the flour, mustard powder, sugar and salt. Make a well in the centre and work in the butter and 1 egg yolk. Knead well. Leave in a cool place for 2 hours then roll out thinly. Cut into fans or triangles. Lay on a greased baking sheet and brush with egg yolk. Bake at 200°C/425°F/gas mark 7 for 7 minutes.

Meanwhile warm the honey and mix in the wholegrain mustard. Brush over the crackers and return to the oven for 5 minutes. Cool on a rack. The crackers can be made in advance and stored in an airtight tin.

Prepare the stock. Roughly chop the onion, garlic, carrots and celery. Place in a large pan with a little oil. Brown lightly. Add the water, sliced mushrooms, cracked peppercorns, bay leaf and thyme. Bring to the boil and then simmer for 30 minutes.

Wash and trim the watercress, shaking off the excess water. Finely chop the shallots, garlic and watercress. Melt the butter in a big pan. Add the shallots, garlic and watercress. Cover and cook for 10 minutes on a low heat. Strain over the stock and stir. Check seasonings. Serve hot with the crackers.

Layered Polenta wrapped in Chard

chard or spinach leaves
a little oil
450g/1lb fine yellow polenta (cornmeal)
400g/14oz tin of plum tomatoes in juice
water
nutmeg
salt
pepper
50g/2oz butter
50g/2oz finely grated Parmesan

Wash the chard. Wilt it in a colander over a pan of boiling water. This will take but a few seconds. Lightly oil a terrine or loaf tin and lay the leaves over the base and sides.

Sift the cornmeal to make sure there are no lumps. Divide equally between two plates. Pass the contents of the tin of tomatoes through a sieve and make the liquid up to 850ml/1½pt. Pour this into a saucepan. Pour the same amount of water into another pan. Season both pans well with nutmeg, salt and pepper. Bring both up to the boil.

Sprinkle one plateful of the polenta into the tomato liquid, stirring well to avoid lumps. When it is smooth, sprinkle the other plateful into the water, stirring well with a clean wooden spoon or spatula. Cook both over a very low heat, stirring from time to time, for twenty minutes. As the mixtures get very thick you will need to beat harder.

Take the tomato mixture off the heat and beat in half the butter. Spread the mixture into the bottom of the prepared terrine, neatly levelling the top. Beat the rest of the butter and the Parmesan into the other polenta mixture then spread it on top of the tomato polenta. Cover with the remaining chard leaves and leave in a cool place overnight.

Bake at 190°C/375°F/gas mark 5 for 20 minutes then turn out and slice.

Alternatively, you can make the polenta like a roulade. Instead of putting the mixture into a terrine, spread the tomato polenta out to a rectangle 25 × 31 cm/10 × 12 in on an oiled silicone paper sheet. Spread the yellow polenta on top, then roll up, Swiss-roll fashion. Do not roll the paper inside. The whole roll can be baked and then sliced or slices can be cut and laid in a gratin dish, dabbed with butter and then grilled.

Note: the polenta will slice more easily if you use a hot, wet knife and clean it between each slice.

Grilled Endive and Orange Butter

9 chicons of chicory
2 sweet oranges
50 g/2 oz unsalted butter
caster sugar

Wash and trim the chicory, discarding any damaged leaves. Cut in half lengthwise. Remove the zest from the oranges and save. Squeeze the oranges. Melt the butter. Mix the butter and juice together.

Arrange the chicory cut side up in a heatproof dish. Dribble or brush the orange butter all over the chicory then sprinkle lightly with sugar. Place under a medium grill until the chicory is tender and there are some nicely caramelised edges. Scatter over some of the orange zest and serve.

Deep-Fried Onion Rings

2 large onions
50g/2oz flour + a little extra
ice-cold water
1 egg white
sunflower oil
salt

Peel the onions and cut into rings about 1cm/½in thick. Dust in the extra flour. Mix the 50g/2oz flour with cold water to the consistency of single cream. Whisk the egg white until stiff then fold through the flour mixture.

Heat the oil to 180°C/350°F. Drop the onion rings in the batter then into the oil. Don't try to fry too many at once. When they are crisp and golden, drain and serve sprinkled with salt.

Rhubarb and Ginger Tiramisù

Sponge
150g/5oz plain flour
1 tsp ground ginger
5 eggs
150g/5oz golden caster sugar

Cream
2 egg yolks
2 tbs caster sugar
450g/1lb Mascarpone
200ml/7fl oz ginger wine

Topping
100ml/3fl oz water
100g/3oz caster sugar
450g/1lb pink, fine rhubarb
1 knobble stem ginger

Sift the flour and ginger together a couple of times. Separate the eggs and whisk the whites until they are softly peaking. Sprinkle with the golden caster sugar and on low speed whip in the yolks. This should be done in a matter of seconds. Fold in the flour and divide between three 20cm/8in lined round cake tins. The mixture will be spread thinly. Bake at 220°C/425°F/gas mark 7 for 5–6 minutes. Cool then peel off the paper.

Line the sides of a deep loose-bottomed 20cm/8in cake tin. Beat together the 2 egg yolks, 2tbs caster sugar and Mascarpone. Pour the ginger wine into a large flat dish. Dip one of the sponge biscuit rounds into the wine and then lay it in the base of the prepared tin. Cover it with a third of the Mascarpone mixture. Dip the next sponge into the ginger wine and repeat the layering process twice, ending with a Mascarpone layer. Smooth neatly then chill very well for at least 2 hours.

For the topping dissolve the caster sugar in the water and boil for 3 minutes. Thinly slice the ginger and add to the barely simmering syrup. Wipe the rhubarb and cut into small chunks, add it to the hot syrup. Leave covered over a low heat for 1 minute. Remove from the heat but do not uncover until cold. Chill well. Spoon over the tiramisù. Unmould and serve.

Menu for March

II

GRAPEFRUIT AND AVOCADO SALAD
WITH HERBED SODA BREAD

BORSCHT-POACHED USZKI WITH SMETANA
DILLED SLAW

GRAPE CARAMEL CUSTARD

Menu for March
II

As spring approaches, a balance is struck between the dark winter flavours in the borscht and the ravioli and the light, citrusy salad. Jaffa 'Sweeties' – the green grapefruits – are also very good and have less of the 'edge' of other grapefruits.

If you are very pushed for time, buy good bread to serve with the salad and make the borscht the night before.

Caramel custard requires chilling so must be made in advance, but too rapid cooling will cause the custard to weep.

SHOPPING LIST

Greengrocery
2 grapefruits – 1 ruby, 1 white
1 lemon
a large bunch of seedless flame grapes
3 ripe avocados
1 small celeriac
lettuce
750 g/1½ lb raw beets
2 large onions
celery
125 g/4 oz dried black mushrooms
50 g/2 oz oyster mushrooms
1 small yellow onion
1 kg/2 lb pointed cabbage
small bunch of chives
fresh mixed herbs – including thyme and a *little* rosemary *or* see GROCERY
fresh dill leaves

Dairy
284 ml/½ pt whipping cream – optional
50 g/2 oz fresh Parmesan
300 ml/½ pt buttermilk *or* soured milk
568 ml/1 pt milk
7 eggs
butter

Grocery

a few small black olives
walnut oil
oil
wheatmeal or wholemeal flour
strong plain flour
baking soda
muscovado sugar
golden caster sugar
dried mixed herbs *or* see GREENGROCERY

allspice
cinnamon sticks
celery salt
black bread
cardamom pod
white pepper
dill seeds
1 vanilla pod
miniature of vodka

SUGGESTED ACTION PLAN

1   Make caramel custard – caramelise grapes.
2   Make borscht.
3   Make pasta and filling.
4   Make bread.
5   Prepare ravioli and cabbage.
6   Whip cream.
7   Assemble salad and serve – have borscht barely simmering.
8   Cook ravioli and cabbage and serve.

Grapefruit and Avocado Salad

2 ripe grapefruits – mix ruby and white ones for a good colour contrast
3 ripe avocados
125g/4oz peeled celeriac
a few small black olives
walnut oil
a lettuce
a small bunch of fresh chives
50g/2oz fresh Parmesan

Peel and segment the grapefruit removing as many pips as possible and all the pith. Put in a large bowl. Peel and stone the avocados and cut into thick slices. Carefully mix with the grapefruit. Cut the celeriac into matchsticks and add to the bowl with the olives. Drizzle over some walnut oil and season well with salt, sugar and black pepper. Pile onto lettuce-lined plates and top with snipped chives and shaved curls of Parmesan. Serve with warm bread.

Herbed Soda Bread

375g/12oz wheatmeal or wholemeal flour
1tsp baking soda
1tbs fresh chopped mixed herbs – include some thyme and a little rosemary or
1tsp dried mixed herbs
½tsp salt
300ml/½pt buttermilk or soured milk

Combine everything in a large bowl, dry ingredients first, and mix to a firm dough. Shape into a large round. Place on a greased baking sheet and slash with a knife to almost cut into six. Bake in a very hot oven 230°C/450°F/gas mark 8 for 35 minutes. Serve still warm.

Celeriac Feuilleté, with Stir-Fried Red Cabbage with Walnuts and Sherried Shiitake Sauce (February I: see pp.31-2)

Red Onion Flamiche - A Valentine's Tarte, with Potatoes Anna Gaurin and Broccoli (February II: see pp.40-1)

Layered Polenta wrapped in Chard, with Deep-Fried Onion Rings

(March I: see pp.48-50)

Borscht-Poached Uszki with Smetana and Dilled Slaw (March II: see pp.57-9)

Quails' Eggs with Leeks and Saffron Sauce (April I: see p.64)

Three Crostini (April II: see p.72)

Borscht-Poached Uszki

Borscht
750g/1½ lb raw beets
2 large onions
a little oil
1 lt/1¾ pt water
allspice
cinnamon sticks
a few celery leaves
celery salt
black pepper
pinch of muscovado sugar
smetana, to garnish

Uszki – Russian Ravioli
125 g/4 oz dried black mushrooms
50 g/2 oz oyster mushrooms
1 small yellow onion
1 cardamom pod
a little oil
1 slice black bread
1 hard-boiled egg
salt
white pepper
125 g/4 oz strong plain flour
1 egg
1 egg yolk
a good pinch of salt

Wash the beets and coarsely grate or chop. A food processor will stop you staining your hands. Also peel and grate or chop the onions. Finely chop the celery leaves. Heat a little oil in a large pan and gently fry the roughly crushed allspice and cinnamon sticks and the celery leaves for a couple of minutes.

Add the beet and onion and fry for ten minutes, stirring. Add the water. Bring to the boil then cover and simmer for 30 minutes.

Remove lid and turn up the heat. Boil hard to reduce by a quarter then strain into a clean pan. Press the pulp with the back of a wooden spoon to extract as much liquid as possible but do not work through the sieve. Season with the celery salt, black pepper and a pinch of sugar.

Pour boiling water onto the dried mushrooms and allow to soak for an hour. Strain the liquid off through a cheesecloth-lined sieve and reserve. Make sure the mushrooms contain no bits of grit then chop finely. Also chop the oyster mushrooms and the onion. Scrape the seeds from the cardamom and crush. Fry gently in a little oil then add the mushrooms and onion and cook over a low heat for 10 minutes. Pour the reserved mushroom liquor over the bread and leave until soft. Chop the hard-boiled egg and add to the mushroom mixture with the bread. Mix well. Season with salt and freshly ground white pepper. Allow to cool.

Combine the flour with the whole egg, egg yolk and salt. Knead well to make a silky smooth dough. Wrap in a tea towel and allow to rest ½ hour. Roll out very thinly and cut into 8 cm/3 in rounds. Place a spoonful of mushroom filling on each round, damp edges, fold over and seal to form crescents.

Poach in the simmering borscht for about 3–5 minutes. Serve with a crescent of dilled slaw and a good spoonful of smetana.

Dilled Slaw

1 kg/2 lb pointed cabbage
a little oil or butter
2 tsp dill seeds
1 lemon
1–2 tbs vodka
fresh dill leaves

Wash the cabbage leaves in very cold water, shake off the excess. Cut off the stalks. Cut into strips approximately 0.5 cm/¼ inch wide, across the leaves. Put the oil or butter into a wok or large pan with the dill seeds and heat. Add the cabbage and combine with the seeds. Shake the pan or stir fry. Cook over a medium flame for 2 or 3 minutes. Add a little lemon juice and the vodka, boil off. Serve immediately, decorated with fresh dill and lemon zest.

Grape Caramel Custard

568 ml/1 pt milk
1 vanilla pod
225 g/8 oz golden caster sugar
a large bunch of seedless flame grapes
4 tbs water
2 eggs + 2 extra yolks
whipped cream – optional

Pour the milk into a saucepan. Split the vanilla pod and scrape out the tiny beans and add to the milk. Stir in 60 g/2 oz of the sugar. Warm gently, do not allow to boil.

Break the bunch of grapes into six neat small bunches. Lightly grease an 18 cm/7 in ring mould and stand in a roasting tin of hot water. Melt the rest of the sugar in the water. When it is dissolved, boil hard until it becomes dark. Dip the grapes into the caramel to coat them. Leave to harden in a cool dry place. Pour enough of the remaining caramel into the ring mould to coat the base and sides.

Beat the eggs and the extra yolks together. Strain the milk and beat gradually into the eggs. Strain the custard into a jug and pour gently into the mould.

Place into a moderate oven 180°C/350°F/gas mark 4 for 35–45 minutes or until a blade slipped into the centre comes out clean. Cool and then chill.

Dip the base of the mould in hot water then invert onto a large serving plate. Decorate with the caramelised bunches of grapes and fill the centre with whipped cream if desired.

Menu for April

I

Quails' Eggs with Leeks and Saffron Sauce

Rustic Tomato Tart
Herbed Baby Roots en Papillotes

Filled Easter Eggs

Menu for April
I

An Easter theme of eggs and nests runs through this springtime menu. If quails' eggs prove impossible to find use 1 pullet's egg per person. The vegetables may be baked all together in a covered casserole if you haven't the time to wrap them in paper.

Well-drained bottled raspberries or blackcurrants are also extremely good in the Easter eggs.

SHOPPING LIST

Greengrocery
450g/1lb cherry tomatoes
18 new potatoes
18 baby turnips
12 baby carrots
3 baby fennel bulbs
a bunch of spring onions
225g/8oz shallots
700g/1½lb leeks
1 bulb garlic
fresh, mixed herbs: thyme, basil *or* rosemary etc.
parsley
a lemon
3 kiwi fruit

Dairy
568ml/1pt full cream milk
125g/4oz butter

2 eggs
18 quails' eggs
4 tbs crème fraîche
300 ml/½ pt double cream
175 g/6 oz Beaufort or Franche Comte cheese

Grocery
wholemeal or granary bread
plain flour
fermipan dried yeast
salt
brown sugar
icing sugar
sugar
poppyseeds
saffron
paprika
3 medium hollow chocolate eggs – or chocolate to make them
200 g/7 oz block white chocolate
400 g/14 oz jar of griottes (cherries) in kirsch

SUGGESTED ACTION PLAN

1   Make dough and leave to rise.
2   Prepare vegetables and wrap in paper.
3   Infuse saffron.
4   Fill Easter eggs, make white chocolate shavings and slice kiwis but don't
    assemble until just before serving.
5   Make tart.
6   Cook leeks, croustades and eggs.
7   Bake vegetable parcels.
8   Serve starter.

Quails' Eggs with Leeks and Saffron Sauce

568 ml/1 pt full cream milk
a good pinch of saffron
700 g/1½ lb leeks
butter
1 tbs flour
6 large slices of good wholemeal or granary bread
18 quails' eggs
paprika

Warm the milk. Crumble the saffron strands and leave to infuse in the milk.

Wash the leeks very well. Cut into 7.5 cm/3 in lengths. Slice in half lengthwise then cut into fine 7.5 cm/3 in strips. Melt a large knob of butter in a big pan. Sauté the leeks until tender. Sprinkle over the flour and cook, stirring, for a couple of minutes. Add the milk and saffron and stir over a low heat as the mixture thickens. Season well. Keep warm.

Remove the crusts from the bread and butter both sides. Press into 7.5 cm/3 in patty tins. Bake for 7 minutes at 220°C/425°F/gas mark 7 until crisp.

Drop the quails' eggs into boiling water for two minutes. Drain and peel.

To serve: place a bread croustade on each plate. Fill with the leek mixture, making it like a nest. Top each nest with three quails' eggs. Dust with paprika.

Rustic Tomato Tart

Dough
340g/12oz plain flour
6g/¼oz fermipan *dried yeast*
a good pinch of salt
1 tsp brown sugar
1 tbs poppyseeds
2 eggs
4 tbs crème fraîche

Filling
225g/8oz shallots
3 cloves garlic
3 tbs fresh, chopped herbs: be sure to include thyme, basil or a little rosemary,
and parsley
2 tbs flour
a good pinch of sugar
salt
pepper
175g/6oz Beaufort or Franche Comte cheese
450g/1 lb cherry tomatoes
a little icing sugar

Sift the flour into a bowl with the yeast, salt and brown sugar. Stir in the poppyseeds. Lightly mix together the eggs and crème fraîche. Make a well in the flour and pour in the egg mixture. Bring together in a soft dough – if the flour is very absorbent you may need a little extra liquid. Knead lightly then place in an oiled bowl in a warm place, until doubled in size. (This takes approximately 1 hour.)

Knock the dough back and allow it to rest whilst preparing the filling.

Very finely chop the shallots and garlic. Mix together with the herbs, flour, sugar, salt and pepper. Grate the cheese and toss it with the shallot mixture. Slice all the tomatoes.

Divide the dough into six balls. Roll each into 20cm/8in rounds. Sprinkle the centre of each with a little of the shallot-cheese mixture, leaving a clear 2.5cm/1in rim. Cover with a neat layer of overlapping tomato slices. Repeat the layering until all is used up. Fold the edges of the dough circles up, neatly pleating them. Bake at 200°C/400°F/gas mark 6 for 20 minutes. Dust with icing sugar and return to the oven for 3 or 4 minutes.

Herbed Baby Roots en Papillotes

18 new potatoes
18 baby turnips
12 baby carrots
3 baby fennel bulbs
a bunch of spring onions
60g/2oz parsley
100g/3½oz butter
a lemon
salt
black pepper

Scrub and trim the potatoes, turnips and carrots. Quarter the fennel bulbs. Put all the prepared vegetables to steam for 7–10 minutes. They should remain *al dente*. Trim and obliquely slice the spring onions. Chop the parsley and cream together with the butter.

Spread out 6 sheets of greaseproof paper. Butter them. Divide the vegetables between them. Scatter over the spring onion. Squeeze over a few drops of lemon juice and season well with salt and pepper. Top with some of the parsley butter. Fold over the edges of the paper to seal. Place in a hot oven for 15 minutes (twenty if you are reheating from cold).

Filled Easter Eggs

*3 medium hollow chocolate eggs (about the size of a number 1 egg – you can
make these yourself if you have time using a good quality chocolate and flexible
moulds available from kitchen shops)*
300ml/½pt double cream
2tbs icing sugar
400g/14oz jar of griottes (cherries) in kirsch
3 kiwi fruit
200g/7oz block white chocolate

With a warm, dry knife halve the chocolate eggs. Whip the cream with the icing sugar until it holds its shape. Drain the cherries and fold into the cream. Fill the chocolate egg shells, smoothing the tops.

Peel and thinly slice the kiwis into rounds. Cut across to make semi-circles and use to edge each dessert plate. Using a potato peeler, shave the white chocolate into a fluttery pile in the centre of each plate – representing the nest. Place the filled egg on top, cut side down. Dribble the kirsch syrup over the kiwi and serve.

Menu for April

II

THREE CROSTINI

SPRING VEGETABLES IN AVGOLEMONO

ARMAGNAC-SOAKED HALVA CAKE WITH PRUNES

Menu for April
II

A short cut on this simple menu is to avail yourself of the wonderful range of Italian bottled antipastos and pastes. Even the most mediocre supermarkets seem to stock at least pesto and tapenade these days and many have roasted peppers, porcini, artichokes, olive pâtés and all manner of exciting things. (Look out for preserved wild hyacinth bulbs!) Ready-made vol au vent cases can be used if necessary.

The grainy halva cake can be made in advance but leave it in the tin so you can warm it before pouring on the syrup.

SHOPPING LIST

Greengrocery
1 bulb of garlic
2 bunches spring onions
1 large yellow pepper
340 g/12 oz broccoli
125 g/4 oz mangetout
175 g/6 oz helda beans
125 g/4 oz oyster mushrooms
60 g/2 oz parsley
3 lemons
1 orange
1 nashi (Asian pear)
fresh basil

Dairy
6 eggs

125 g/4 oz unsalted butter
150 g/5 oz Mozzarella
50 g/2 oz Gorgonzola
284 ml/½ pt double or single cream

Grocery
ciabatta – Italian olive oil bread
sun-dried tomatoes in olive oil
100 g/3 oz black olives
capers
olive oil
450 g/1 lb puff pastry – or butter, flour and lemon to make
225 g/8 oz pruneaux d'Agen
125 g/4 oz hazelnuts
light brown sugar
caster sugar
semolina
baking powder
a stick of cinnamon
miniature of Armagnac

SUGGESTED ACTION PLAN

1   Make pastry or defrost shop-bought.
2   Make the cake.
3   Prepare the vegetables.
4   Roll the pastry.
5   Prepare the crostini.
6   Bake the pastries.
7   Cook the vegetables, make the sauce, fill pastries – keep warm.
8   Grill the crostini, serve.

Three Crostini

18 slices of ciabatta – Italian olive oil bread
1 clove of garlic
1 large yellow pepper
150g/5oz Mozzarella
1–2 sun-dried tomatoes in olive oil
100g/3oz black olives
1 tbs capers
2 cloves garlic
1 nashi (Asian pear)
50g/2oz Gorgonzola
fresh basil

Toast the ciabatta slices lightly on both sides. Rub with a cut clove of garlic.

Grill and skin the pepper. Chop, discarding the seeds. Mix with a little olive oil. Drain the Mozzarella and pull into strips. Cut the sun-dried tomato into tiny shards. Mix with the pepper. Top six of the slices with the peppers and the Mozzarella.

Stone the olives and purée coarsely with half the capers and 1 clove of garlic. Spread the resultant paste over six more slices. Deep fry the remaining capers as a garnish, if liked.

Cut the nashi into quarters and remove the core. Chop into small dice. Cut the Gorgonzola into equally small pieces and mix into the nashi with a crushed clove of garlic. Pile on the remaining six ciabatta slices.

Place all the crostini under the grill until sizzling. Serve one of each variety on a plate with a fresh sprig of basil.

Spring Vegetables in Avgolemono

450g/1lb puff pastry – shop-bought or home-made
4 egg yolks
4 cloves of garlic
2 bunches spring onions
2 tbs olive oil
340g/12oz broccoli
125g/4oz mangetout
175g/6oz helda beans
125g/4oz oyster mushrooms
60g/2oz parsley
2 lemons
200ml/7fl oz water
salt
black pepper

Divide the pastry into six pieces and roll each out to a square 15 x 15 cm/6 x 6in. Lay them, well spaced, on a lightly greased baking tray. Score a line around each square, 1cm/½in in from the edge. Lightly impress a criss-cross pattern of lines on the inner squares. Chill.

Beat the egg yolks very well with a pinch of salt. Use a little to brush the top of the pastry squares, avoiding the edges and the cuts. Place in a hot oven, 225°C/425°F/gas mark 7, for 15–20 minutes until well risen, crisp and brown.

Peel and slice the garlic and spring onion. Put to fry gently in the olive oil. Break the broccoli into tiny florets and slice the stalks. Slice the mangetout, beans and mushrooms. Chop the parsley. Add all these to the pan with the juice of 1 lemon and the water. Season well with salt and pepper. Bring to the boil and cook for 3 minutes. Drain, reserving the cooking liquor.

Pour the hot cooking liquor onto the egg yolks, whisking well. Pour the mixture back into the pan, over the vegetables, stirring well over a low heat until thickened. Do not boil or it will turn into scrambled eggs.

When the pastries are cooked, run a knife around the score lines and lift off the central square. Fill the cavity with the lemon-sauced vegetables, replace the lid and decorate with a thin twist of lemon, cut from the remaining fruit. Serve.

Armagnac-Soaked Halva Cake with Prunes

225 g/8 oz pruneaux d'Agen
a stick of cinnamon
the finely grated rind and juice of 1 lemon
4 tbs water
125 g/4 oz light brown sugar
50 ml/2 fl oz Armagnac
125 g/4 oz hazelnuts
125 g/4 oz unsalted butter
125 g/4 oz caster sugar
2 eggs
175 g/6 oz semolina
2 tsp baking powder
1 orange
single or double cream, to serve

Put the prunes, cinnamon, lemon juice, water and brown sugar in a pan. Bring to the boil, cook for 2 minutes then pour on half the Armagnac and leave to steep.

Toast the hazelnuts until they begin to colour slightly and give off an irresistible aroma. Tip into a clean cloth and rub off the skins. Cool then finely grate.

Beat together the butter, caster sugar and lemon rind until fluffy and light. Lightly whip the eggs and remaining Armagnac together then gradually beat it into the butter mixture. Sift the semolina with the baking powder and combine with the hazelnuts. Using a spoon fold into the mixture. Put in a silicone paper-lined 20 cm/8 in tin. Bake at 220°C/425°F/gas mark 7 for 10 minutes then reduce the heat to 180°C/350°F/gas mark 4 for half an hour.

Put the warm cake on a plate, discard the cinnamon stick and arrange the prunes on the top. Pour over any remaining cooking liquor and decorate with swirls of orange zest. Serve with single or double cream.

Menu for May

I

TAGLIATELLE WITH ROCKET AND PINENUTS

VEGETABLE STRUDEL
GRILLED CHERRY TOMATOES
CUCUMBER DOLCE AGRODOLCE

MUSCAT SABAYON WITH STRAWBERRIES
AND GINGER THINS

Menu for May
I

May can be a glorious month, full of the promise of summer. If it is hot, you might like to make some minor alterations to the menu: serve a tomato salad, make a lighter filling for the strudel (more herbs, more cheese and no cabbage) and have it cold. The strudel dough is time-consuming – use filo or puff pastry around the same filling if you are rushed.

The strawberries are usually from Spain in May and taste better than early glasshouse crops. The gentle warmth of the sabayon heightens the flavours too. If the weather is not so kind, divide the strawberries between gratin dishes and grill the tops of the sabayon instead. The ginger thins can be made a week ahead of time and kept in an airtight tin.

SHOPPING LIST

Greengrocery
125 g/4 oz rocket leaves
1 large Spanish onion
1 bulb garlic
225 g/8 oz mushrooms
225 g/8 oz spring greens or primo cabbage
24 cherry tomatoes – red and yellow if possible
1 very large or 2 smaller cucumbers
225 g/8 oz small deep-red strawberries
1 lemon
mint
thyme
chives
lemon balm leaves/borage flowers to decorate – optional

Dairy
12 eggs
60 g/2 oz fresh block Parmesan
225 g/8 oz cottage cheese
75 ml/2½ fl oz sour milk or buttermilk (or sour fresh milk with a squeeze of lemon)
125 g/4½ oz butter

Grocery
Type '00' strong plain flour
plain flour
olive oil
60 g/2 oz pinenuts
caraway seeds
white peppercorns
caster sugar
sugar
icing sugar
½ bottle Muscat de Frontignan or similar
ground ginger
paprika

SUGGESTED ACTION PLAN

1 Make strudel dough.
2 Make pasta dough.
3 Make strudel filling.
4 Prepare cucumber, get tomatoes ready.
5 Roll and cut pasta ribbons.
6 Make strudel.
7 Hull strawberries, measure sabayon ingredients (cook just before serving).
8 Cook pasta, fry pinenuts and rocket, grill tomatoes.
9 Serve.

Tagliatelle with Rocket and Pinenuts

110g/4oz '00' strong plain flour
a good pinch of salt
1 egg
1 egg yolk
3 tbs olive oil
60g/2oz pinenuts
125g/4oz rocket leaves
salt
black pepper
60g/2oz fresh block Parmesan

Sift the flour and salt. Make a well in the centre and add the egg and egg yolk. Work into a stiff dough and knead well for 10–15 minutes until smooth, silky and no longer sticky. Allow to rest for 20 minutes then roll out very thinly and cut into ribbons of desired width. Leave until needed on floured tea towels or on pasta airers. When required boil a large pan of salted water. Add the pasta and 1 tbs of oil. Cook until *al dente* – the fresher it is the less time it will take; check after 3 minutes.

Dry fry the pinenuts until lightly golden. Add the remaining olive oil and the rocket. When the rocket has just wilted in the oil, toss in the freshly cooked and drained tagliatelle and toss with salt and freshly ground black pepper. Serve immediately with curls of Parmesan, shaved off with a potato peeler.

Vegetable Strudel

75 ml/2½ fl oz sour milk or buttermilk (or sour fresh milk with
a squeeze of lemon)
100 g/3½ oz butter
1 egg
200 g/7 oz '00' strong plain flour
a good pinch of salt
black pepper
1 large Spanish onion
2 cloves garlic
225 g/8 oz mushrooms
2 tbs oil
225 g/8 oz spring greens or primo cabbage
3 hard-boiled eggs
a small bunch of chives
225 g/8 oz cottage cheese
1 tsp caraway seeds
paprika

Put the milk or buttermilk into a small saucepan with 15 g/½ oz of the butter. Warm until the butter melts. Leave to cool to blood heat. Melt the remaining butter in a separate pan. Beat in the egg. Sift the flour with the salt and plenty of freshly ground black pepper. Make a well in the centre and pour in the milk mixture. Mix then knead until a smooth dough is formed – this will take about 10 minutes. Brush with melted butter, cover and leave in a warm place for 1 hour.

Finely shred the onion, garlic and mushrooms and cook briefly in the oil until just softened. Cool. Shred the cabbage, discarding any tough stalk. Shell and chop the hard-boiled eggs. Chop the chives and mix with the cottage cheese.

Work some flour into a clean old tablecloth or a pair of tea towels. Flour a pastry board. Place the dough on the board and roll out as thinly as possible using a lightly floured rolling pin. When it does not seem to be stretching any further, pick up the dough sheet and transfer it to the cloth. Using the backs of your hands under the dough, gently stretch it, little by little further and further out. Move around your dough if possible – if not, turn the cloth around to reach all sides of the dough. You should be able to stretch the dough to approximately 90 × 90cm/36 × 36in. Don't worry if it is slightly less but aim for at least 80 x 80cm/32 × 32in.

Brush the dough all over with melted butter and sprinkle with the caraway seeds. Scatter on the onion mixture and top with the cabbage. Top this with the cottage cheese and chives. Then roll up, using the cloth underneath to help you. Bend around into a circle and ease onto a greased baking tray. Brush all over with butter and bake at 200°C/400°F/gas mark 6 for 25–30 minutes. Dust with paprika before serving. Fill the centre with grilled cherry tomatoes.

Grilled Cherry Tomatoes

24 cherry tomatoes – if you can get a mixture of red and yellow
so much the better
1 tbs olive oil
salt
pepper
sugar

Spread the tomatoes out in a flat heatproof dish. Drizzle with the oil and sprinkle with the salt, pepper and sugar.

Place under a moderate grill, turning once until slightly browned.

Cucumber Dolce Agrodolce

125 g/4 oz caster sugar
1 lemon
150 ml/5 fl oz water
a small handful of mint
white peppercorns
a little thyme
1 very large or 2 smaller cucumbers

Put the sugar into a small pan. Peel a large piece of the lemon zest and add it to the sugar with the juice of the lemon and the water. Slowly bring to the boil then boil hard until syrupy. Chop the mint and add to the hot syrup with the coarsely ground peppercorns and the thyme.

Before serving cut the cucumber into 5 cm/2 in chunks. Slice these chunks into slender wedges. Heat in the syrup until piping hot and serve with a little of the syrup.

Muscat Sabayon with Strawberries

250 g/8 oz small deep-red strawberries
6 egg yolks (put aside 1 egg white for the ginger thins)
250 g/8 oz caster sugar
250 ml/8 fl oz Muscat de Frontignan or similar (Moscatel di Valencia makes an
acceptable cheap alternative)
mint or lemon balm leaves/borage flowers to decorate – optional

Hull the strawberries and keep at room temperature – chilling deadens their flavour. Whisk the egg yolks and sugar until ribboning – the mixture falls from the whisk in a broad 'ribbon'. Whisk in the Muscat and set the bowl over a pan of simmering water. (Pour into a double boiler if you prefer.) Continue whisking until the mixture is thickened and doubled in bulk.

Quickly layer up strawberries and sabayon in 6 tall glasses. Decorate with the leaves and flowers and serve immediately.

Ginger Thins

25 g/1 oz plain flour
25 g/1 oz melted butter
50 g/2 oz icing sugar
1 egg white – saved from the sabayon making
1 tsp ground ginger
a pinch of finely ground black pepper

Line a baking sheet with silicone paper. Using a whisk, place all the ingredients in a bowl and beat lightly to make a smooth batter.

Drop teaspoonfuls of batter onto the lined baking sheet, drawing them out into long tongue-shaped biscuits – the batter should be evenly spread and well spaced: no more than 6 to a tray.

Bake at 200°C/400°F/gas mark 6 for 4–5 mins. Carefully and immediately remove from the tray. Cool.

Menu for May

II

MANGO SALAD

SAVOURY PALMIERS

EGYPTIAN NEW POTATOES WITH SOURED CREAM
AND CHIVES

MIXED LEAVES

ELDERFLOWER CHARLOTTE

Menu for May
II

There is nothing heavy in this menu. Colours, flavours and textures are light.
There are mangoes in season all year round. They vary enormously, all having
their own characteristics, in the same way that a Cox's Orange Pippin is nothing
like a Granny Smith. In May imports are likely to be from Kenya and India.

Homegrown elderflowers abound everywhere on building lot or country
roadside. Make your own cordial by steeping heads in syrup or buy it in health
food stores and supermarkets.

Gelozone, the vegetarian gelatine, is easy to work with but do not boil it. Full
instructions appear on the packet. It does not have exactly the same properties as
gelatine but it works perfectly well in this context.

SHOPPING LIST

Greengrocery
1 small red onion
3 spring onions
1 medium onion
1 bulb garlic
1 cauliflower
675 g/1½ lb Egyptian new potatoes
a good bunch of chives
flat parsley
Little Gem lettuce
cabbage-type lettuce
feuilles de chêne
radicchio
chervil

lovage
sorrel
ginger root
3 large oranges
2 lemons
2 barely ripe mangoes
6 kiwi fruit *or* 225 g/8 oz strawberries
elderflowers/lemon balm leaves – optional
6 fresh red chillies – optional

Dairy
3 eggs
150 g/5 oz fromage blanc
340 g/12 oz petit Suisses – or 'high' fat fromage frais
2 tbs soured cream

Grocery

sugar
caster sugar
acacia honey
flour
oil
olive oil
walnut oil
sesame oil – untoasted
450 g/1 lb puff pastry – or butter, flour
   and lemon to make

Gelozone
pink peppercorns
black peppercorns
coarse sea salt
mustard seeds
turmeric
paprika
1 bottle elderflower cordial –
   home-made or shop-bought

SUGGESTED ACTION PLAN

1 Make the cake and then the charlotte.
2 Make the puff pastry or defrost shop-bought.
3 Prepare the onion and mango.
4 Scrub and cook the potatoes.
5 Make palmiers and filling.
6 Prepare mixed leaves.
7 Finish mango salad and serve.

Mango Salad

1 small red onion
3 spring onions
1 lemon
2 barely ripe mangoes
salt
black pepper
1–2 tsp freshly grated ginger
3 large oranges
sugar
75 ml/3 fl oz untoasted sesame oil
flat-leaved parsley
6 fresh red chillies – optional, for garnish

Peel and thinly slice the red onion. Chop the spring onions and place both in a large bowl. Squeeze over the juice of the lemon. Peel and slice the mangoes. Add to the onion and sprinkle with 1 tsp salt, a good grinding of black pepper and the ginger. Leave to stand 1 hour.

Cut the oranges in half (vandyking – zigzag cuts – if liked) and remove the flesh. Squeeze and measure 75 ml/3 fl oz of the juice. Sweeten with a good pinch of sugar. Whisk the juice with the oil until emulsified. Drain the mangoes and fill the reserved orange halves. Drizzle with the orange dressing. Chop the parsley and scatter it over the salads. Garnish with a spring onion or chilli flower.

Savoury Palmiers

450g/1 lb puff pastry (home-made or good quality shop-bought)
1 tsp pink peppercorns
1 tsp black peppercorns
1 tsp coarse sea salt
½ tsp mustard seeds
1 egg white
1 medium onion
2 cloves garlic
1 tbs oil
½ tsp turmeric
1 cauliflower
150g/5 oz fromage blanc

Roll out the pastry to a square 30 x 30cm/12 x 12in. Cut into 24 strips. Roll both ends of the strip in towards the middle, commencing with a 2.5cm/1in fold. This will give you a sort of Incan-style capital 'B' shape. Repeat with remaining 23 strips. Lay them, well spaced, on lightly greased baking trays. Coarsely grind the peppercorns, sea salt and mustard seeds. Lightly whip the egg white until it is just breaking up. Brush the palmiers with the egg white then sprinkle with the peppercorn mixture. Bake at 225°C/425°F/gas mark 7 for 10–15 minutes until crisp and golden. Cool on a rack.

Very finely chop the onion and garlic and cook slowly in the oil, with the turmeric. When softened add the cauliflower, broken into florets. Cook, covered, over a low heat until soft. Purée and season well. Stir in the fromage blanc. Sandwich pairs of palmiers with the cauliflower mixture and reheat in a hot oven for 7 minutes before serving.

Egyptian New Potatoes
with Soured Cream and Chives

675 g/1½ lb Egyptian new potatoes
3 cloves garlic
2 tbs olive oil
salt
pepper
a good bunch of chives
2 tbs soured cream
paprika

Scrub the potatoes well. Peel the garlic. Place them both in a heavy lidded pan (a cast iron skillet is ideal but a heatproof casserole will work). Pour over the oil and turn the potatoes about in it as if dressing a salad. Put the lid on and place over a low heat. Shake the pan from time to time but do not open the lid. Cook for 30 minutes. Sprinkle well with salt and pepper. Add the chopped chives and soured cream. Mix and dust with paprika to serve.

Mixed Leaves

a combination of salad leaves and herbs including:
Little Gem lettuce; cabbage-type lettuce; feuilles de chêne; radicchio; parsley;
chervil; lovage; sorrel
walnut oil

Wash, dry and tear the leaves. Mix them together well in a large bowl. Just before serving, drizzle with a little walnut oil and toss.

Elderflower Charlotte

2 eggs
90g/3 oz caster sugar + a little extra to dust paper
60g/2 oz flour
1 tbs hot water
1 bottle elderflower cordial – home-made or shop-bought
2 tsp Gelozone
6 kiwi fruit or 225g/8 oz strawberries
340g/12 oz petit Suisses (if unavailable, use 'high' fat fromage frais,
but it must be strained for 2 hours in muslin)
2 tbs acacia honey
1 tsp finely grated lemon rind
elderflowers/lemon balm leaves (decoration – optional)

Whisk the eggs and sugar in a bowl over hot water until very light and thick. (A warmed bowl and an electric mixer will also work.) Fold in the sifted flour. Then fold in the hot water. Pour into a silicone paper-lined 18 × 28 cm/7 in × 11 in Swiss roll tin. Bake at 225°C/450°F/gas mark 7 for 7 minutes. Turn out onto a sugared paper on a cooling rack and leave until cold. Then cut six circles of sponge to fit the top (not the base – watch out for any flaring) of 7.5 cm/3 in ramekins.

Dilute the elderflower cordial to taste with water (some brands are stronger than others, some are ready-diluted and you won't need any extra water) to make 550 ml/1 pt. Place in a pan with the Gelozone. Whisk until dissolved then heat until steaming. Do not boil. Allow to cool. Beat the petit Suisses with the honey and the lemon rind.

Peel the kiwi fruit and slice or slice the strawberries. When the elderflower jelly has cooled a little but is not set, pour a little into the base of 6 x 7.5 cm/3 in ramekins. Arrange some fruit in the base of the ramekins and, dipping the slices in the jelly, around the sides. Fill with the petit Suisses mixture, levelling the top. Cover with a sponge circle and dribble over the remaining jelly. Chill well for at least 6 hours.

Loosen the edges with a round-bladed knife then turn out to serve decorated with elderflowers and lemon balm leaves.

Note: the sponge cake trimmings can be reduced into crumbs, mixed with melted good dark chocolate and liqueur and rolled into balls for home-made truffles. Dust in icing sugar or cocoa or dip in white chocolate and serve with coffee as petits fours.

Menu for June

I

Artichoke-Stuffed Artichokes

Black Tower Pancakes with a
Spring Onion and White Wine Reduction

New Potatoes

Bunches of Carrots

Whole Broad Beans

Eskimo Nellies

Menu for June
I

There are some big, definite flavours in this menu but it is not heavy. Artichokes have a pronounced flavour of their own and here it is merely accented with garlic, lemon and coriander.

If tiny broad beans are unavailable, buy 1 kg/2½ lb of large ones and shell and peel them to reveal that exquisite bright green. Alternatively, as that is rather a fiddly job, serve sugar snap peas or fine beans.

To save time, make the parfait well in advance or use a good shop-bought ice cream instead.

SHOPPING LIST

Greengrocery
12 globe artichokes – don't buy any that are papery-looking
1 bulb garlic
2 lemons, thin skinned and softish – ensure they are unwaxed
750 g/1½ lb slender broad beans
2 bunches baby carrots
750 g/1½ lb tiny new potatoes
1 kg/2 lb spinach
2 bunches spring onions
bunch of chives – Chinese chives are longer and stronger for tying up the carrots
fresh coriander
7 large ripe peaches
500 g/1 lb red currants

Dairy
6 eggs

284 ml/½ pt double cream
150 ml/5 fl oz yoghurt
450 g/1 lb Ricotta
125 g/4 oz unsalted butter

Grocery
extra virgin olive oil
125 g/4 oz buckwheat flour
60 g/2 oz plain flour
baking powder
muscovado sugar
caster sugar
small box Amaretti – tiny Italian bitter almond macaroons
bread – white or wholemeal to taste
½ bottle medium dry white wine
nutmeg

SUGGESTED ACTION PLAN

1 Make peach parfait.
2 Cook artichokes.
3 Make filling for pancakes.
4 Start sauce, add butter just before serving.
5 Make redcurrant coulis.
6 Finish artichokes and prepare vegetables.
7 Make pancakes and stack towers.
8 Scald peaches and whisk meringue ready but do not assemble 'nellies' until after the main course.

Artichoke-Stuffed Artichokes

12 globe artichokes
2 lemons
4 cloves garlic
1 tsp ground coriander
30g/1 oz fresh coriander
very good olive oil
black pepper
salt
sugar
2 slices of good bread – white or wholemeal according to preference

Wash the artichokes very well. Trim the stalk close to the base and discard any damaged leaves. Pack into a large pan. Pour over boiling water and the juice of one lemon. Bring back to the boil. Cover and cook for 40 minutes. Drain the artichokes, standing them upside down on a clean towel.

Peel away the leaves, reserving the biggest and best on six plates. Arrange them in a starburst pattern, tips outward. Discard the tiny leaves and scrape away the central thistly 'choke', leaving the cup-shaped hearts. Place one heart in the middle of each plate. Purée the remaining six hearts with 2 cloves of garlic and 1 tbs olive oil until smooth. Season with salt, black pepper and a good pinch of ground coriander. Pipe or spoon the purée into the hearts on the plates.

Make the bread into crumbs, add a teaspoon of finely grated lemon rind, salt and freshly ground black pepper. Spread out on a baking tray and drizzle with a little olive oil. Toast under a low grill, turning frequently until nicely browned. Leave to cool.

Squeeze the remaining lemon into a screw-topped jar, add twice as much oil as there is juice. Finely chop the coriander leaves, discarding the stalks, then put in the jar. Add a good pinch of sugar and salt and some black pepper.

Just before serving top the purée with the crumbs. Shake the dressing in the jar until it emulsifies and then dribble it over the leaves.

Black Tower Pancakes

Filling
1 kg/2 lb fresh spinach
olive oil
2 cloves garlic
450 g/1 lb Ricotta
nutmeg
black pepper
salt

Batter
2 eggs, separated
150 ml/5 fl oz plain yogurt
125 g/4 oz buckwheat flour
60 g/2 oz plain flour
1 tsp baking powder

Prepare the filling: wash the spinach, shake dry and tear into small pieces. Heat a tablespoon of oil in a large pan, over a low heat. Add the peeled, crushed garlic and the spinach. Turn about as if dressing a salad. Cook until the spinach is very tender, turning up the heat to boil off any excess liquid. Add half the Ricotta and season well with freshly grated nutmeg, black pepper and salt. Reheat when required.

Combine the yolks, yoghurt and remaining Ricotta and beat well. Sift the flours together with the baking powder and a pinch of salt and gradually beat in the yolk/yoghurt mixture. Whisk the egg whites until stiff then fold through the batter.

Heat a lightly oiled griddle or heavy frying pan. Form little pancakes, about 7.5 cm/3 in across, with a good tablespoon of batter. Cook until set and nicely browned on one side then flip over and cook the other side. Keep warm whilst cooking the remaining batter.

Layer up with the spinach mixture, making six separate towers, on a heatproof plate. Bake at 190°C/375°F/gas mark 5 for 15 minutes.

Spring Onion and White Wine Reduction

2 bunches spring onions
2 cloves garlic
½ bottle medium dry white wine
125 g/4 oz unsalted butter
2 tsp oil
salt
black pepper

Chop the spring onions and garlic and place in a heavy-bottomed pan with the oil. Cook covered over a low heat until softening. Add the wine and season well with salt and pepper. Bring up to the boil and simmer for 20 minutes. Turn up the heat to reduce by half. Cut the butter into tiny dice and keep very cold.

Just before serving: reheat the sauce to a barely trembling simmer, whisk in the butter a little at a time. DO NOT STOP WHISKING whilst adding the butter and keep on a low heat. Serve as soon as all the butter has been incorporated.

Vegetables

750g/1½lb tiny new potatoes
2 bunches baby carrots
750g/1½lb young broad beans – no thicker than your finger
a bunch of chives
1 tbs olive oil
150ml/5fl oz water

Wash the potatoes and carrots well – there shouldn't be any need to scrape but if the skins have begun to thicken, scrub off. Trim the carrots' root ends and the greenery, leaving 2cm/¾in of green shoots. Divide into six bundles and tie the tops together with a chive. Cook the potatoes in a little water for no more than 20 minutes – they may be tender in 15, depending on size. Cook the carrots in a steamer over the potatoes. Top and tail the broad beans, removing any strings. Stew in a covered pan with the oil, water and remaining chopped chives until tender – about 15 minutes.

Eskimo Nellies

3 large ripe peaches

Parfait
4 large ripe peaches
4 eggs, separated
125 g/4 oz golden caster sugar
284 ml/½ pt double cream
a small box Amaretti – about 75 g/2½ oz

Meringue
2 egg whites
125 g/4 oz caster sugar

Coulis
500 g/1 lb redcurrants
caster sugar

Scald four of the peaches and skin them. Halve and stone them. Either work through a sieve or purée in a food processor. Separate the eggs. In a bowl over hot water, beat the yolks and sugar until very light, thick and creamy. Whisk the egg whites until stiff and whip the cream until mounding. Fold the purée through the egg yolks, next fold in the cream. Then fold in the egg whites and lastly crush the Amaretti and fold them through. Put into a lidded container and freeze until firm.

Liquidise the redcurrants – reserving six perfect sprays – just enough to break them up, then work through a sieve. Sweeten to taste remembering that the sauce is accompanying meringues – err on the sharp side. Stir until the sugar dissolves.

Whisk the egg whites for the meringue until stiff then whisk in the sugar, a little at a time. Place in a forcing bag with a large nozzle. Scald and peel the remaining peaches. Halve and stone them. Place cut side up on a large heatproof dish.

On each peach place a scoop of frozen parfait, pushing it well into the peach. Quickly pipe the meringue all over the parfait, ensuring there are no gaps. Flash in the hottest oven or under a grill until the meringue is lightly browned, 2–3 minutes maximum. Serve immediately on plates with a puddle of the coulis and the spray of whole redcurrants – set off with a lemon geranium leaf if liked.

Menu for June

II

ASPARAGUS IN A CHEESE TUILE WITH LIME HOLLANDAISE
AND DEEP-FRIED LIME TWISTS

MILLE FEUILLES OF AUBERGINE
WITH A ROASTED PEPPER CONFETTI

MINTED PEAS AND LETTUCE WITH CRÈME FRAÎCHE

CHARRED COURGETTES

GRILLED PINEAPPLE WITH LOQUAT ICE
AND STRAWBERRY PURÉE

Menu for June
II

The English asparagus season is so short that you should be as generous as you can. Look upon a kilo as the minimum to buy for six people. If you are looking to cut corners, serve the asparagus with a simple melted butter sauce with a squeeze of lime and some good bread.

First class shop-bought hummus, thinned with a little stock, can be used to layer the mille feuilles and will save more time. Avoid any that is brown and crusty at the edges as it will be past its best.

If loquats are unavailable, make (or buy) a mango and passion fruit ice.

SHOPPING LIST

Greengrocery
12 little yellow and green courgettes
1 kg/2 lb bundle of asparagus – look for slender green stems
2 very large aubergines
1 onion
1 bulb garlic
1 small red pepper
1 small yellow pepper
1 small green pepper
500 g/1 lb tiny fresh peas
3 Tom Thumb lettuces
2 limes
1 small lemon
1 medium pineapple
250 g/8 oz deep red strawberries
500 g/1 lb loquats (Japanese medlars)

mint or lemon balm leaves
rosemary

Dairy
30 g/1 oz butter
150 g/5 oz unsalted butter
100 ml/3½ fl oz crème fraîche
4 eggs
30 g/1 oz block Parmesan

Grocery
olive oil
sesame oil
plain flour
fine yellow cornmeal
dry mustard
white pepper
300 g/12 oz dried chick peas
ground cumin
cayenne – optional
sugar
caster sugar
brown sugar

SUGGESTED ACTION PLAN

1   Soak chick peas.
2   Make loquat ice.
3   Make tuiles, prepare courgettes.
4   Make chick pea filling, roast peppers, make confetti.
5   Purée strawberries, grill pineapple.
6   Make lime twists.
7   Make hollandaise, cook asparagus.
8   Fry aubergine, cook vegetables.

Asparagus in a Cheese Tuile with Lime Hollandaise and Deep-Fried Lime Twists

1 kg/2 lb bundle of asparagus – look for slender green stems

Tuiles
30 g/1 oz butter
30 g/1 oz plain flour
15 g/½ oz fine yellow cornmeal
2 (No 3) egg whites
a good pinch of mustard powder
30 g/1 oz fresh grated Parmesan or other hard dry cheese
salt
pepper

Deep-fried lime twists
1 lime
olive oil

Hollandaise
125 g/4 oz unsalted butter
1½ tbs lime juice
4 tbs boiling water or light, wine-based stock
3 egg yolks
salt
pepper

Melt the butter. Sift the flour, cornmeal, mustard powder, salt and pepper together into a bowl. Using a whisk, mix in the egg whites and butter. Beat lightly to make a smooth batter. Line two baking trays with silicone paper. Place three tablespoonfuls of batter on each tray, ensuring they are widely spaced. Smooth each out to a 10 cm/4 in round. Sprinkle with a little grated Parmesan. Bake for 6 minutes at 220°C/425°F/gas mark 7. Remove from the tray immediately and, using a clean tea towel, gently press around a rolling pin, giving the classic pantile shape. Leave on the pin to cool.

Before squeezing the lime for its juice, pare off 6 long narrow strips. It is easy to do this with a potato peeler. Make sure there is no white pith. In a small pan heat some oil to a depth of 2cm/¾in. Have ready a metal sieve over another pan. Toss the lime peel into the hot oil, allow to cook a few seconds then quickly pour the oil through the sieve into the clean pan, leaving the peel in the sieve. Shake gently to remove any excess oil then tip out onto some kitchen paper.

Make hollandaise sauce: melt the butter and keep warm. Combine the lime juice with the water or stock in a small pan. Season with salt and pepper. Bring to the boil and reduce by half. Strain into a double boiler and when cooled to blood heat beat in the egg yolks. Heat, stirring continually until the mixture begins to thicken. Turn off the heat and gradually whisk in the butter. Serve at once. If the mixture does begin to curdle, all is not lost. Beat it, little by little, into a fresh egg yolk.

Trim the asparagus and wash well. Tie into six bundles and stand upright in a tall, deep pan. If you do not have an asparagus kettle, try improvising with a double boiler (invert the inner pan over the top as a very high domed lid) or a pressure cooker (stand the spears in 4-sided metal graters to hold them up in such a wide pan). They should be cooked in 8–10 minutes, drain well, then serve each bundle with a tuile around it and a little mound of hollandaise, decorated with the lime twist.

Mille Feuilles of Aubergine
with Roasted Pepper Confetti

300g/12oz dried chick peas – also sold as garbanzos
1 onion
4 cloves garlic
sesame oil
1–2 tsp ground cumin
2 very large aubergines
plain flour
cayenne – optional
1 small red pepper
1 small yellow pepper
1 small green pepper
salt
pepper

Soak the chick peas overnight. Boil in water until tender. If you want a mild garlic flavour also cook the peeled cloves of garlic in the water. Drain, reserving the cooking water. Purée or mash.

Chop the onion and garlic and fry until golden in 2 tbs sesame oil and the cumin. Add the chick pea purée and thin to the consistency of custard with the cooking water. Stir well over a low heat. Season to taste with salt and pepper. Keep hot.

Slice the aubergines obliquely to give thin ovals. Save the end knobbles. You need at least 24 but preferably 30 slices. Coat both sides lightly in plain flour seasoned with salt, pepper and cayenne. Just before serving, fry in very hot oil until crisp and brown. Drain and layer up with the chick pea mixture – do not use too much filling between each crisp aubergine 'leaf'. Serve surrounded with roasted pepper confetti.

Halve the peppers and remove the seeds and pith. Place cutside down on a grill pan with the ends of the aubergine. Put under a hot grill until the skins blacken and blister and the aubergine is cooked. Scrape away the peppers' papery skins and cut them and the aubergine into tiny dice. Place in a clean jar and cover with a little oil. Shake to make sure all are covered. Spoon a little around the base of each aubergine mille feuilles.

Minted Peas and Lettuce with Crème Fraîche

500g/1 lb tiny fresh peas
3 Tom Thumb lettuces
a good pinch of sugar
a little white pepper
a knob of unsalted butter
100ml/3½fl oz crème fraîche

If the peas are older they will need a little initial cooking before adding the lettuce.

Wash the lettuces, shake dry and cut into strips. Melt the butter. Add the lettuce and the peas and season with the sugar and pepper. Cook covered for a bare 5 minutes. There should be enough moisture in the lettuce to steam the peas. If, extraordinarily, there is not, add a tablespoon of water, *but no more*. Stir in the crème fraîche and adjust the seasoning. Warm through. Serve, sprinkled with chopped herbs if desired.

Charred Courgettes

12 small thin courgettes – if possible a mixture of green and yellow
olive oil
salt
pepper
rosemary

Score lines spiralling around the courgettes. Brush lightly with oil and season well with salt and pepper. Strew with a few rosemary needles. Leave in a cool place for at least 1 hour. Place under a hot grill, turning to cook evenly. Allow to 'scorch' briefly. Serve.

Grilled Pineapple with Loquat Ice and Strawberry Purée

100g/3½oz caster sugar
300ml/½pt water
500g/1lb loquats (Japanese medlars)
2 egg whites
250g/8oz deep red strawberries
1 small lemon – if required
1 medium pineapple
brown sugar
some small mint or lemon balm leaves

Dissolve the caster sugar in the water and simmer for 4 minutes. Add the halved loquats and simmer for a further 2 minutes. Liquidise. Pass through a sieve, rubbing to push through the loquats. Cool. Whisk the egg whites until stiff then fold through the loquat syrup. Freeze, taking out of the freezer from time to time, to beat hard as the mixture becomes slushy. If you have an ice-cream maker, churn freeze the mixture.

Hull the strawberries – reserving some for added decoration if wished – and purée. Check flavour, adjusting with sugar or lemon juice as required.

Peel the pineapple and cut into thick slices. Sprinkle lightly with brown sugar and place under a hot grill until nicely browned. Cool.

To serve: soften the loquat ice slightly by leaving in the fridge for half an hour. Using 2 large teaspoons, form little egg-shapes of the ice. Place three 'eggs' on each pineapple slice and puddle the strawberry purée around. Set off with the mint or lemon balm leaves.

Note: you can serve the pineapple ungrilled if you prefer, but make sure it is really ripe.

Menu for July

I

Port-Poached Peaches and Dolcelatte Ice Cream

Courgette Charlotte
Sorrel Sauce
Glazed Baby Onions
Baked Beetroot

Raspberry and Chocolate Cream Layers

Menu for July
I

I was amazed to discover from Caroline Liddel and Robin Weir's *ICES* that savoury ice creams have been around for more than a hundred years. I have long been fond of them, having devised several for my first book, *NEITHER FISH NOR FOWL – Meat-free Eating for Pleasure*. I am indebted to *ICES* for the inspirational addition of cloves – don't leave them out, they are essential in rounding out the flavours. Later in the year when pears arrive in quantity they can be used instead of peaches.

The charlotte can be made as one big terrine if preferred and sliced to serve. Cook for twice as long if you decide to do this. The meringues can be made in advance and stored in an airtight tin or frozen.

SHOPPING LIST

Greengrocery
225 g/8 oz courgettes
340 g/12 oz Spanish onions
1 bulb garlic
4 spring onions
450 g/1 lb tiny onions
125 g/4 oz tomatoes
10 large sorrel leaves
1 kg/2 lbs beetroot
125 g/4 oz fresh raspberries
2 lemons
6 firm peaches

Dairy
284 ml/½ pt milk
568 ml/1 pt double cream
200 ml/7 fl oz strained Greek yoghurt
50 g/2 oz butter
5 eggs
175 g/6 oz Dolcelatte

Grocery

olive oil
white bread
flour
sugar
caster sugar
cocoa powder
100 g/3½ oz fine dark chocolate
allspice berries
dried red chillies

black peppercorns
mustard seeds
a stick of cinnamon
bay leaf
cloves
miniature of vodka
½ bottle ruby port
ground ginger

SUGGESTED ACTION PLAN

1 Make meringues.
2 Make ice cream.
3 Poach peaches.
4 Prepare vegetables, bake beetroot.
5 Make charlottes.
6 Prepare creams but don't assemble meringues until just before serving.
7 Make sorrel sauce.
8 Cook onions.
9 Reduce syrup, soften ice in fridge.
10 Peel beets, serve peaches and ice cream.

Port-Poached Peaches and
Dolcelatte Ice Cream

Peaches
6 firm peaches
284 ml/½ pt ruby port
4 allspice berries
2 dried red chillies
4 black peppercorns
a few mustard seeds
a stick of cinnamon
125 g/4 oz sugar

Ice Cream
284 ml/½ pt milk
284 ml/½ pt double cream
2 cloves
1 bay leaf
4 black peppercorns
4 egg yolks
175 g/6 oz Dolcelatte – you could also use St Agur or Gorgonzola
60 ml/2 fl oz vodka

Scald the peaches and remove the skins. Pour the port into a deep casserole with the allspice, chillies, peppercorns, mustard seeds and cinnamon. Add half the sugar. Heat stirring until the sugar has dissolved. Put the peaches into the port. Cover and simmer until tender. Leave to infuse.

Heat the milk and cream with the 2 cloves, bay leaf and peppercorns. Do not boil but allow to infuse for 10 minutes. Beat the egg yolks well then strain the hot milk on to them, stirring constantly. Return to the pan and cook over a low heat until the custard has thickened. Cut the cheese into small dice and stir into the custard until melted. Stir in the vodka.

Pour into an ice-cream maker and churn freeze for 20 minutes *or* pour into a freezer tray and freeze until mushy. Beat well and freeze again quickly until nearly firm.

Slice the peaches and arrange on the plates. Add the remaining sugar to the port and boil up until thick and syrupy. Pour a little over the peaches. Add a scoop of the dolcelatte ice cream and serve.

Courgette Charlotte

225 g/8 oz courgettes
340 g/12 oz Spanish onions
1 clove garlic
1 tbs olive oil
200 ml/7 fl oz strained Greek yoghurt
1 egg
2 tbs white breadcrumbs
1 tbs flour
salt
pepper

Thinly slice the courgettes, lengthwise. Blanch, drain and pat dry. Lightly oil 6 ramekins. Line the ramekins with the courgette slices. Chop any remaining courgette quite small.

Chop the onion and garlic and cook, with any leftover courgette, in the oil until soft but not coloured. Purée in a liquidiser or food processor with the yoghurt, egg, breadcrumbs and flour. Blend until smooth then season well with salt and plenty of black pepper.

Fill the ramekins, levelling the tops neatly. Stand in a bain-marie and bake at 180°C/350°F/gas mark 4 for 25 minutes. Leave to stand 5 minutes then turn out and serve.

Sorrel Sauce

2 cloves garlic
4 spring onions
2 tbs oil
125 g/4 oz tomatoes, peeled, seeded and chopped
10 large sorrel leaves
salt
pepper
a squeeze of lemon

Finely chop the garlic and spring onions. Cook slowly until soft in the oil, add the tomatoes and cook, covered, for a further 5 minutes over a low heat. Shred the sorrel leaves and add to the pan. Stir and take off the heat. Leave covered for 5 minutes. Season to taste with salt, pepper and lemon if necessary. Serve just warm.

Glazed Baby Onions

450 g/1 lb tiny onions
150 ml/5 fl oz water
3 tbs sugar
a large knob of butter

Peel the onions and trim the ends. Place in a pan with the other ingredients. Bring to the boil, cover and allow to simmer gently until tender. Depending on size this may be 10–20 minutes. Uncover and boil off any remaining liquid, shaking the pan to avoid sticking.

Baked Beetroot

1 kg/2 lb beetroot
butter
salt
pepper
ground ginger
lemon juice

Scrub the beetroot and bake, in their skins, until tender, 1–2 hours depending on size at 180°C/350°F/gas mark 4. Peel and cut into dice. Toss in butter and season with salt, pepper, ground ginger and lemon juice.

Raspberry and Chocolate Cream Layers

3 egg whites
150g/6oz caster sugar
30g/1oz cocoa powder
100g/3½oz fine dark chocolate
284ml/½pt double cream
125g/4oz fresh raspberries

Whisk the egg whites until softly peaking. Gradually whisk in the sugar until very stiff. Sift the cocoa and fold in carefully. Pipe or spoon 18 × 7.5cm/3in rounds onto silicone paper-lined baking trays. Bake in a very cool oven 110°C/225°F/gas mark ¼ until dried and firm – about 1½ hours. Leave to cool and store in an airtight tin.

Break the chocolate in half and reserve one half for making chocolate curls to decorate. Melt the remaining chocolate in a bowl over hot water. Cool.

Whip the cream until mounding. Divide between 2 bowls. Combine one part of the cream with the chocolate and the other with the raspberries. Place a meringue circle on each plate and cover with the chocolate cream. Top with another meringue and cover with the raspberry cream. Put a final meringue on the top and shave over the chocolate curls. Serve.

Menu for July

II

CHILLED CHEESE SOUFFLÉ WITH GOOSEBERRY JELLY
AND MELBA TOAST

STUFFED TOMATOES
GOLDEN SALSA
GRILLED FENNEL
FILLED FOCACCIA

COLETTE'S CHERRY SOUP WITH BRIOCHE CROÛTONS

Menu for July
II

This is a lovely cool summery meal. If the weather is not glorious you can serve the tomatoes hot. Almost all the menu can be prepared in advance, including the focaccia, freezing it when you have shaped and filled the dough.

Colette's Cherry Soup is an adaptation of one of the French writer's recipes. She had a passion for the cooking of her native Burgundy. Similar fruit soups are found across Northern Europe.

SHOPPING LIST

Greengrocery
2 medium onions
1 bulb garlic
1 kg/2 lb spinach
125 g/4 oz oyster mushrooms
6 large tomatoes
3 bulbs of fennel
2 medium sweet yellow peppers
225 g/8 oz gooseberries
2 lemons
1 kg/2 lb morello cherries
a few sprigs of rosemary
borage flowers

Dairy
300 ml/10 oz crème fraîche
75 g/3 oz unsalted butter
3 eggs

Muscat Sabayon with Strawberries and Ginger Thins (May I: see pp.82-3)

Savoury Palmiers, with Egyptian New Potatoes with Soured Cream and Chives and Mixed Leaves (May II: see pp.89-90)

Port-Poached Peaches and Dolcelatte Ice Cream (July I; see pp 114-15)

Stuffed Tomatoes on Golden Salsa, with Grilled Fennel and Filled Focaccia

(July II: see pp.123-5)

225 g/8 oz Caerphilly cheese
100 g/3½ oz fresh Parmesan
vanilla ice cream – optional

Grocery
Gelozone
bread
brioche
plain flour
strong plain flour
instant dried yeast
60 g/2 oz black olives
olive oil
nutmeg
saffron
a cinnamon stick
golden granulated sugar
salt
black pepper

SUGGESTED ACTION PLAN

1 Make soufflé and chill.
2 Marinate the fennel.
3 Make the stuffed tomatoes.
4 Make the dough.
5 Toast bread, grill the fennel.
6 Make the gooseberry jelly.
7 Make the focaccia.
8 Make the soup.
9 Make the salsa, bake the focaccia.
10 Fry the croûtons, unmould the soufflés.

Chilled Cheese Soufflé with Gooseberry Jelly

300ml/10oz crème fraîche
1½ + 1 tsp Gelozone – vegetarian gelatine
3 eggs
225g/8oz Caerphilly cheese, finely grated
225g/8oz gooseberries
salt
pepper

Prepare six small ramekins by tying a double thickness of baking paper around each, coming 4cm/1½in above the rim of the dishes.

Place the crème fraîche in a pan and sprinkle with 1½ tsp of the Gelozone. Whisk in until dissolved, then heat until almost boiling. Separate the eggs and beat the egg yolks until light. Whisk in the scalding crème fraîche and stir in the cheese. Season well. Whisk the egg whites until stiff then fold through the cheese mixture. Fill the prepared dishes, rapping them lightly to settle the contents. Fill to not quite the top of the papers. Put in a cold place to set for at least 2 hours.

Liquidise the gooseberries then sieve. Place in a pan then sprinkle on the remaining 1 tsp of Gelozone. Stir well until dissolved then heat until steaming. Leave to cool and when on the point of setting cover the tops of the soufflés with the gooseberry jelly. Chill well for another hour, stand the ramekins on plates and carefully peel away the paper. Serve with two fingers of melba toast.

Melba Toast

3 large slices of bread

Toast the bread on both sides. Cut in half, then split the slices by inserting a knife between the toasted surfaces. Toast the newly exposed 'other' sides, but watch carefully as they are liable to burn.

Stuffed Tomatoes

2 medium onions
3 cloves garlic
olive oil
1 kg/2 lb spinach
nutmeg
125 g/4 oz oyster mushrooms
60 g/2 oz black olives
30 g/1 oz breadcrumbs
6 large tomatoes

Finely chop the onion and garlic and put in a large pan with a little oil. Cook slowly until beginning to soften. Wash and shake the spinach dry. Tear into small pieces discarding any stringy stalks. Add to the onions and mix well. Cook until you have a soft mass. Season well with nutmeg.

Slice the oyster mushrooms and cook briefly in a very little oil, in a covered pan. Stone and finely chop the olives. Mix together the mushrooms, olives and breadcrumbs.

Scald the tomatoes and peel. Slice off the tops and scoop out the insides. Use for another purpose. Fill the tomato cavities with the spinach and mushroom mixtures in neat layers. Replace the tops.

The tomatoes can be reheated to serve but I prefer them cold with a warm focaccia.

To serve: invert each tomato onto a plate and surround with the golden salsa.

Golden Salsa

1 clove garlic
a pinch of saffron
2 medium sweet yellow peppers
1 tbs freshly squeezed lemon juice
2 tbs pale olive oil
salt
pepper
borage flowers

Crush the garlic and place in a bowl with the saffron strands. Pour on a teaspoon of boiling water and leave to stand whilst you grill and skin the peppers. Discard the seeds and chop well. Combine with the garlic and saffron. Add the lemon juice and oil. Season then mix well. Divide between the plates. Add the tomatoes and decorate with the borage flowers.

Grilled Fennel

3 bulbs of fennel
1 lemon
olive oil
salt
black pepper

Quarter the fennel bulbs lengthwise and place in a heatproof dish. Squeeze over the lemon juice and drizzle on olive oil. Dust well with salt and pepper and then turn the fennel pieces about until all are coated. Leave to stand at least half an hour. Place under a hot grill and turn occasionally. Grill until tender. Cool to just warm or chill before serving.

Filled Focaccia

350g/12oz strong plain flour
7g/¼oz instant dried yeast
1 tsp salt
3 tbs olive oil
approx 200ml/7fl oz warm water
100g/3½oz fresh Parmesan
a few sprigs of rosemary
crushed garlic – optional

Sift the flour, yeast and salt together. Make a well and pour in the oil and most of the water. Mix to a soft dough adding more water if needed. Knead well for 10 minutes then leave in an oiled bowl in a warm place until well risen and doubled in bulk.

Shave or grate the Parmesan. Oil a large baking tray.

Knock the dough back and knead again lightly. Divide in half and roll or press the dough out to two large circles – 0.5cm/¼in thick. Place one circle on the tray. Cover it with the cheese and top with the other round of dough. Seal the edges together, pinching well between finger and thumb. Press a few sprigs of rosemary into the top of the dough. Brush with a little extra oil and sprinkle with a little salt. Leave in a warm place for about a quarter of an hour and then bake at 230°C/450°F/gas mark 8 for about 15 minutes. Dribble on a little more oil and serve on a large board. Cut in wedges.

Crushed garlic can be put in the centre with the Parmesan if liked.

Colette's Cherry Soup with Brioche Croûtons

1 kg/2 lb morello cherries
a cinnamon stick
75 g/3 oz golden granulated sugar
200 ml/7 fl oz water
75 g/3 oz unsalted butter
1 tbs plain flour
black pepper
2 thick slices of day-old brioche
icing sugar – optional
ground cinnamon – optional

Stone the cherries. Tie the pits in a piece of muslin and hit with a hammer to break a few up. Place in a tightly covered pan with the cherries, cinnamon stick, sugar and water. Bring to the boil and simmer for 15 minutes.

In a clean pan, melt 50g/2oz of the butter and stir in the flour. Cook over a low heat without colouring. Gradually stir in the cooking liquid from the cherries. Keep stirring until the mixture comes to the boil. Add the cherries and turn the heat to a simmer. Cook a further 10 minutes. Check flavour and add more sugar if required. A grinding of black pepper makes an interesting addition. Serve hot with the croûtons. A small dollop of really good vanilla ice cream makes a lovely contrast.

To make the croûtons, cut the brioche into small cubes and fry them in the remaining butter until crisp and golden. Dust in icing sugar and ground cinnamon if liked. If preferred, Amaretti can be used instead.

Menu for August

I

FRENCH BEAN SAMOSAS
WITH MINTED YOGHURT SAUCE

UNDEY VINDALOO
COURGETTE FOOGATH
SAG KOFTA
SAFFRON RICE
FRESH NECTARINE CHUTNEY
PESHWARI NAN

PISTACHIO KULFI WITH MANGO SAUCE

Menu for August
I

Just the shopping list for this veritable banquet looks daunting – but don't be put off, much of the length is in the variety of spices needed. If you wanted you could choose to leave out one or two dishes. All of the curries (including the filling for the samosas) can be prepared in advance and reheated. The kulfi too can be made a week or so previously and left frozen. The chutney can be left in the fridge overnight so only last minute jobs are detailed in the action plan.

If you are fortunate enough to have one of those rare warm sultry August nights, consider moving your feasting outside. Spread rugs and cushions and serve from big brass trays. Don't forget masses of candles and sweet-smelling incense.

SHOPPING LIST

Greengrocery
450g/1lb French beans
450g/1lb onions
1 bulb garlic
1 sweet red pepper
1 fiery red pepper
2 small green chillies
225g/8oz tomatoes
450g/1lb spinach
225g/8oz floury potatoes
450g/1lb small courgettes
1 large ripe mango
1 sweet orange
340g/12oz ripe nectarines
3 limes

fresh turmeric root
ginger root
coriander leaves

Dairy
150 ml/5 fl oz double cream
75 ml/3 fl oz milk
125 g/4 oz butter *or* ghee
275 g/10 oz plain yoghurt
6 eggs

Grocery
a cinnamon stick
cumin seeds
coriander seeds
dried chillies
black onion seeds
mustard seeds
bay leaves
ground cinnamon
ground coriander
cayenne – optional
paprika – optional
ground turmeric
ground cumin
garam masala
saffron
cardamom pods
aniseeds
dried lemon grass
rosewater
ground almonds
desiccated coconut
raisins
60 g/2 oz shelled pistachios
self-raising flour
instant dried yeast

wholemeal flour – optional
gram (chick pea) flour – optional
cornflour or arrowroot
muscovado sugar
caster sugar
icing sugar
sugar
oil
sesame oil
25 g/1 oz tamarind paste
white wine vinegar
340 g/12 oz basmati or patna rice
410 g/14 oz tin unsweetened condensed milk

SUGGESTED ACTION PLAN

Make in advance:
kulfi
samosa filling
vindaloo sauce (but don't add the eggs – have them ready hard-boiled though)
foogath
koftas – but fry at the last minute
pepper sauce
chutney
mango purée

On the day:
1   Make nan dough – prepare filling.
2   Make samosa dough and roll and shape samosas.
3   Make yoghurt sauce.
4   Cook rice.
5   Fry samosas and serve. Leave rice tightly covered.
6   Bake nan, fry koftas and reheat curries (adding eggs).

French Bean Samosas

Filling
½ tsp cumin seeds
1 tsp coriander seeds
1 small dried chilli
1 medium onion
2 cloves garlic
2.5 cm/1 in piece ginger
2 tbs oil
a few coriander leaves
½ tsp black onion seeds
450 g/1 lb French beans
salt
1 tsp ground turmeric
2 tbs ground almonds
60 ml/2 fl oz water

Dough
225 g/8 oz plain flour or half and half plain and wholemeal
1 tsp salt
3 tbs melted ghee or oil
80–100 ml/3–4 fl oz very warm water
oil – soya or peanut

Dry roast the cumin and coriander seeds with the chilli. Grind as finely as possible.

Peel and finely chop the onion and garlic. Grate the ginger. Fry the onions, garlic and ginger in the oil with the chopped coriander leaves until nicely browned. Add the spices and cook for a few minutes. Add the beans, a good pinch of salt, the turmeric, almonds and 60 ml/2 fl oz water. Stir and cook slowly until tender. Allow to cool.

Sift the flour(s) with 1 tsp salt. Rub in the ghee or oil. Add enough of the warm water to make a firm dough. Knead it for 10 minutes until smooth. Pinch off a large walnut-sized piece, keeping the rest of the dough covered, and roll out to a

13–15 cm/5–6 in diameter circle. Cut the round in half. Use each half to form a cornet, sealing the overlapping edge with water. Fill with some of the French beans mixture and seal the top edge, pinching the sides together. Repeat with the rest of the dough.

Deep fry in hot oil until a deep golden.

Minted Yoghurt Sauce

100 g/3½ oz fresh mint leaves
1 medium onion, roughly chopped
2 cloves garlic
1 tsp salt
a large pinch of sugar
½ tsp cumin
some freshly ground black pepper
1 tbs lime juice
200 g/7 oz plain yoghurt
cayenne or paprika – optional

Place everything except the yoghurt in a blender and process until smooth. Add the yoghurt and whizz to blend. Serve, dusted with a little cayenne or paprika if liked.

Undey Vindaloo

25 g/1 oz tamarind paste
200 ml/7 fl oz boiling water
2 tsp white wine vinegar
3 cloves garlic
1 cm/½ in piece peeled root ginger
1 small fresh chilli, deseeded
1 tsp salt
1 tsp cumin seeds
1 tsp mustard seeds
225 g/8 oz onion
2 tbs oil
2 bay leaves
1 tsp ground cinnamon
1 tsp ground turmeric
½ tsp ground coriander
1½ tbs muscovado sugar
pepper
6 hard-boiled eggs

Place the tamarind paste in a bowl and pour over the boiling water. Stir and leave to stand. Blend together the vinegar, garlic, ginger, chilli, salt, cumin and mustard seeds to make a paste. If your processor won't cope with small quantities use a mortar and pestle. Finely chop the onion and cook it in the oil with the bay leaves until golden. Stir in the paste and cook stirring for a couple of minutes. Add the cinnamon, turmeric, coriander and sugar. Strain the tamarind liquid into the pan, stirring well. Slide in the halved eggs and simmer gently until thick.

Courgette Foogath

2 cloves garlic
125 g/4 oz onion
fresh turmeric root
ginger root
1 small dried red chilli
2 tbs oil
1 bay leaf
450 g/1 lb small courgettes
1 lime
a good pinch of salt
plenty of black pepper
1 tbs chopped coriander leaves

Crush the garlic and chop the onion. Grate enough turmeric and ginger to make 2 tsp. Fry the garlic, onion, turmeric and ginger and chilli in the oil with the bay leaf. When softened add the courgettes cut into 5 cm/2 in length. Squeeze over the lime juice and season with salt and pepper. Cook until just tender – about 10 minutes. Sprinkle with coriander before serving.

Sag Kofta

Vegetable balls
450 g/1 lb spinach
2 cloves garlic
1 small green chilli
a knob of butter or ghee
225 g/8 oz floury potatoes, cooked and mashed
1 tsp garam masala
salt
gram (chick pea) or plain flour
oil for frying

Sauce
1 small onion
2 cloves garlic
1 sweet red pepper
1 fiery red pepper
1 tbs oil
225 g/8 oz chopped tomatoes

Wash the spinach and remove any stalks. Tear into pieces. Finely chop the garlic and green chilli. Cook the spinach, garlic and chilli in the butter over a low heat for 10 minutes. Turn up the heat and using a chopping motion with a wooden spoon turn into a dryish purée.

Mix into the potato with the garam masala and a good pinch of salt. The mixture should be quite firm – if not work in a little flour. Divide into 18 balls, rolling them between the palms of your hands. Dust in flour and deep fry until crisp. Serve with the hot red sauce.

Finely chop the onion, garlic and peppers. Cook in the oil until softened. Add the tomatoes and cook stirring to make a thick, mushy sauce. Season well with salt and pepper.

Saffron Rice

a good pinch of saffron strands
1 tbs very hot water or milk
340g/12oz basmati or patna rice
a knob of butter or 1 tbs ghee
a bay leaf
a cinnamon stick
3 cardamom pods
850ml/1½pt boiling water
½tsp salt

Put the saffron to soak in the hot water or milk. Rinse the rice until the water runs clear. Drain well. Put the butter or ghee into a heavy-bottomed pan with a tight-fitting lid. Fry the bay leaf, cinnamon and cardamom for a couple of minutes then stir in the rice. Pour on the boiling water, add the salt and cover tightly. Cook over a low heat for 10 minutes. Stir in the saffron. Re-cover and cook for a further 5 minutes. Turn off the heat and leave for 5 minutes, then fluff and send to the table.

Fresh Nectarine Chutney

1 tsp mustard seeds
½ tsp black onion seeds
1 tbs sesame oil
1 tsp freshly grated ginger
340 g/12 oz ripe nectarines
1 lime
1 tsp cornflour or arrowroot
raisins – optional

Pop the seeds in a dry pan then add the oil and ginger. Cook for a minute but do not let the ginger burn. Add the diced, stoned nectarines and cook briefly. Squeeze the lime and mix the juice smoothly with the cornflour or arrowroot. Pour onto the nectarines and stir until thickened and clear. Cool then chill. If liked raisins may be added.

Peshwari Nan

75 ml/3 fl oz milk
a good knob of butter or 1 tbs ghee
75 g/3 oz plain yoghurt
1 tsp sugar
300 g/10 oz self-raising flour
1 tsp salt
7 g/¼ oz fermipan instant dried yeast
60 g/2 oz ground almonds
30 g/1 oz desiccated coconut
½ tsp ground cinnamon
1–2 cardamom pods
a few chopped raisins
rosewater

Scald the milk and add the butter or ghee. Mix well with the yoghurt and sugar and cool to just warm. Sift the flour with the salt and yeast. Make a well in the centre. Pour in the milk mixture and knead well until no longer sticky. Leave to rise in a greased bowl.

Mix together the almonds, coconut and cinnamon. Scrape the seeds from the cardamom pods and crush. Add to the almonds. Stir in the raisins and a little rosewater.

When the dough has doubled in size, knock it back and form into 12 balls. Roll each out and top with a little of the almond mixture. Fold over the dough, seal and roll out lightly.

Place on a heavy baking sheet and put in a very hot oven 230°C/450°F/gas mark 8 for 4–5 minutes. When they have puffed and speckled, turn them over and cook 2 minutes on the other side.

Pistachio Kulfi with Mango Sauce

410g/14oz tin unsweetened condensed milk
4 cardamom pods
1 tsp aniseeds
1 tsp dried chopped lemon grass
3 tbs caster sugar
150ml/5 fl oz double cream
1 tsp rosewater
60g/2oz shelled pistachios
1 large ripe mango
1 sweet orange
icing sugar

Pour the condensed milk into a small saucepan. Scrape the cardamom seeds out of the pods and crush. Add them to the milk with the aniseeds and lemon grass. Heat until steaming. Stir in the caster sugar. Take off heat and stir until dissolved. Allow to cool down slowly. When cold, mix in the double cream and rosewater. Strain into a container and freeze until mushy. Finely chop the pistachios and mix well into semi-frozen mush. Divide between 6 dariole moulds. Freeze until firm. Allow only 10 minutes in the fridge before serving, to soften slightly. Serve with a puddle of mango sauce.

Peel the mango and rub the flesh through a sieve. Add enough orange juice to make the right consistency. Sweeten to taste with icing sugar.

Note: churn freezing in an ice-cream maker is inappropriate.

Menu for August

II

BARBECUED SWEETCORN

CHARGRILLED PIZZETTE
AUBERGINES ON A STICK
GRILLED CAMEMBERT AND PEACHES
GREEN SALAD

TOFFEE BANANAS WITH MASCARPONE

Menu for August
II

Barbecues used to be seen as belonging to an exclusively carnivorous world but, fortunately, things have changed. The pleasures of cooking and eating outside are too good to miss.

There are effectively two action plans given here. The first is the preparation stage, the second the cooking. Serve the food as it is ready to eat. The secret of a successful barbecue is to have everything ready to hand, before you start, and then to relax and enjoy a very informal meal.

Crème fraîche on pizza came from a trip to a pizzeria in Auch, prefecture town of the Gers. Topping options there also included foie gras, really a case of local traditions mixing with new imports.

SHOPPING LIST

Greengrocery
1 small chilli
1 bulb smoked garlic
1 bulb garlic
2 large onions
6 large sweetcorn on the cobs
750g/1½lb baby aubergines
2 tomatoes
1 cos lettuce
1 butterhead lettuce
baby spinach
lovage or celery leaves
fennel (the herb)
mint

rosemary
thyme
fresh basil
3 limes
6 large bananas
500 g/1 lb peaches
1 lemon

Dairy
125 g/4 oz butter
100 g/3½ oz crème fraîche
small block Parmesan *or* sec goat's cheese
1 Camembert *or* 2 Neufchâtel en Bray cheeses
340 g/12 oz Mascarpone

Grocery
salt flakes
strong plain flour
dried yeast
olive oil
nutmeg
2 Mars Bars
tomato purée
wholegrain Meaux mustard
honey
walnut oil

SUGGESTED ACTION PLAN

Preparation:
1 Marinate the aubergines.
2 Make the dough.
3 Light the barbecue. It is not ready to use until the flames die down and the coals are white-hot. Use woody cuttings of rosemary and lavender to get it going rather than lots of firelighters which stink.
4 Wrap the filled bananas.
5 Have ready the pizzette toppings.
6 Prepare mustard for peaches.
7 Have limes and butter ready.
8 Make salad.

Cooking:
1 Barbecue sweetcorn.
2 Cook pizzette.
3 Grill aubergine.
4 Glaze and grill peaches, then cheese, serve with salad.
5 Cook bananas, serve with Mascarpone.

Barbecued Sweetcorn

1 small chilli
1 clove smoked garlic
black pepper
125 g/4 oz butter
6 large sweetcorn on the cobs
salt flakes
3 limes

Deseed the chilli and chop it very finely with the garlic. Add a few twists of coarsely ground black pepper. Work them all into the butter, combining well. Fashion into a log in some greaseproof paper. Chill well, then slice into 12.

Grill the sweetcorn over very hot charcoal until tender and lightly browned in patches. Serve each cob sprinkled with crushed salt flakes and accompanied by 2 lime quarters and 2 slices of butter.

Chargrilled Pizzette

350g/12oz strong plain flour
7g/¼oz fermipan-type dried yeast
1 tsp salt
200ml/7fl oz warm water
2 tbs olive oil
2 large onions
1–2 cloves garlic
a little oil
100g/3½oz crème fraîche
salt
pepper
nutmeg
2 tomatoes
Parmesan or sec goat's cheese
fresh basil

Prepare the dough by sifting the flour, yeast and salt together and pouring in the oil and most of the water. Knead well, adding a little more water if necessary, to form a smooth, elastic dough. Leave in an oiled bowl in a warm place to rise for 45 minutes. Punch the dough back and knead again. Form into eight balls. Roll each out thinly. Place on lightly floured greaseproof paper and leave in the fridge until needed (you can do this up to 2 hours in advance).

Finely chop the onion and garlic and cook slowly in a very little oil until softened. Stir in the crème fraîche, season well with salt, pepper and nutmeg. Thinly slice the tomatoes. Shave the Parmesan or *sec* into a pile of fluttery pieces.

Brush the grill with a little oil. Put it over very hot charcoal. Place rounds of dough on it. Cook until nicely browned on one side then flip over. Spread over the onion mixture. Tear up some basil and scatter it over. Layer on the tomatoes and scatter with the cheese shavings.

Aubergines on a Stick

750g/1½lb baby aubergines
2 cloves garlic
3 tbs tomato purée
1 lemon
olive oil
thyme
rosemary
salt
pepper
sugar

Cut enough green sticks (about the size of a pencil) for the aubergines. Strip off the bark.

Trim the stalk end and then score lines through the aubergine skin. You can spiral them around or simply make shallow cuts from top to bottom every centimetre or so. Peel and crush the garlic. Combine with the tomato purée, 2 tbs of lemon juice and a little grated rind, a tablespoon of olive oil and some thyme. Season with salt, pepper and a generous pinch of sugar.

Impale each aubergine on a stick, then brush thickly all over with the tomato mixture. Scatter over some sprigs of rosemary then leave in a cool place for a couple of hours.

To cook, place on a lightly oiled grill over hot charcoal, sticks pointing outwards, off the grill. Turn frequently until cooked through, about 7 minutes.

A good mild curry paste can be used instead if preferred.

Grilled Camembert and Peaches

1 whole slightly underripe Camembert (you can use a couple of the pretty
Neufchâtel en Bray heart-shaped cheeses if you prefer)
4 tbs wholegrain Meaux mustard
4 tbs honey
500 g/1 lb peaches

Combine the mustard and honey. Halve and stone the peaches, brush with the mustard. Place on the grill and turn once when the mustard glaze has browned. Keep warm whilst grilling the cheese on both sides. It blackens lightly and 'puffs' when ready. It will be deliciously hot and runny when you cut it open. Serve with the peaches.

Green Salad

1 cos lettuce
1 butterhead lettuce
a few small spinach leaves
a few lovage or celery leaves
a few sprigs of fennel
a few mint leaves
walnut oil

Wash and dry the lettuces and tear them up. Place in a big bowl. Chop the spinach, lovage, fennel and mint leaves. Toss through the lettuce and then drizzle with a little walnut oil, just before serving.

Toffee Bananas with Mascarpone

6 large bananas
2 Mars Bars
Mascarpone

Carefully slit the banana peels from top to bottom, without cutting the bananas inside. Slice the Mars Bars very thinly and slip the slices into the banana skins. Wrap each banana in a foil packet and place on the barbecue for 10 minutes – 5 minutes each side (this assumes that by the pudding course your barbecue is no longer white-hot). Serve, handing Mascarpone separately – not haute cuisine perhaps but 'good bad food' as once described in a Sunday newspaper.

Menu for September

I

FENNEL SOUFFLETTES
WITH ORANGE BUTTER SAUCE

LEEK AND SHALLOT TARTE TATIN
BRAMBLE SAUCE
SHREDDED KALE
CELERIAC AND POTATO RÖSTI

CHOCOLATE FEUILLETÉS WITH CAFÉ AU LAIT CREAM

Menu for September

I

Rich red, oranges, golds and green: all the colours of autumn are picked up in this menu. Later in the month use elderberries in place of blackberries for the sauce. If you need to save time, buy chocolate thins for the feuilletés but make sure they are not minted.

SHOPPING LIST

Greengrocery
225 g/8 oz fennel (1 good-sized bulb)
1 kg/2 lb leeks
450 g/1 lb shallots
1 bulb garlic
2 large potatoes
1 medium celeriac
ginger root
450 g/1 lb kale
2 kumquats – optional
4 large sweet oranges
250 g/8 oz blackberries
1 lemon
12 physalis (Cape gooseberries)

Dairy
4 eggs
250 g/8 oz butter
50 g/2 oz unsalted butter
150 g/6 oz Emmental cheese
284 ml/½ pt double cream

Grocery
plain flour
olive oil
toasted sesame oil
light muscovado sugar
golden caster sugar
icing sugar
1 cinnamon stick
4 allspice berries
4 black peppercorns
1 small dried red chilli pepper
nutmeg
50 g/2 oz shelled hazelnuts
150 g/6 oz plain chocolate
100 g/4 oz good white chocolate
coffee or a miniature of Kahlua (Mexican coffee liqueur)
½ bottle red wine

SUGGESTED ACTION PLAN

1 Make chocolate leaves.
2 Make the pastry.
3 Cook leeks and shallots.
4 Prepare rösti.
5 Make sauce bases – finish immediately before serving.
6 Make pudding and layer.
7 Cook fennel and purée.
8 Cook tarte, prepare kale (but cook when dishing main course).
9 Cook soufflettes.
10 Cook rösti, finish sauces, serve soufflettes.

Fennel Soufflettes

225 g/8 oz fennel (1 good-sized bulb)
2 cloves of garlic
1 tbs olive oil
3 eggs
salt
pepper
6 orange half shells reserved from the sauce-making
2 kumquats – optional

Trim the fennel, setting aside any feathery tops for garnishing. Chop the rest roughly. Peel and chop the garlic. Place the fennel and garlic with the oil in a covered pan and cook over a low heat until soft.

Purée then pass through a sieve. Dry the purée out over a low heat, stirring to prevent sticking.

Separate the eggs and beat the yolks into the hot purée off the heat. Season well.

Whisk the egg whites until stiff. Fold into the fennel purée, then spoon into the orange halves. Stand the filled oranges in a deep heatproof dish. Pour a little water into the bottom of the dish. Bake at 220°C/425°F/gas mark 7 for 15 minutes until puffed and nicely browned.

To serve: stand on individual plates with a crescent of orange butter sauce, a garnish of kumquat slices and a flourish of fennel greenery.

Orange Butter Sauce

4 large sweet oranges
1 lemon
1 shallot, chopped
50g/2oz cold unsalted butter, cut into small dice

Squeeze the oranges and lemon. Reserve six of the empty orange halves, cleaning them out as thoroughly as possible.

Place the shallot in the pan with the juices. Bring to the boil and boil hard until only 4tbs of liquid remain in the pan. Turn the heat down to a minimum. Whisk in the butter a little at a time. Do not allow the sauce to boil. As you whisk the sauce will thicken. When all the butter has been added, season and serve immediately. This sauce is delicate and cannot be reheated. If you must keep it warm, add 1tbs cream to the reduced juices before adding the butter. Keep the sauce hot then for a little while in a Thermos or bain-marie.

Leek and Shallot Tarte Tatin

225 g/8 oz plain flour
175 g/6 oz butter
1 egg yolk
75 ml/3 fl oz ice-cold water
½ tsp salt
1 kg/2 lb leeks
375 g/13 oz shallots
1 tbs oil
2–3 tbs light muscovado sugar
salt
pepper
150 g/6 oz Emmental cheese

Sift the flour onto a board and make a well in the centre. Cut 150g/5oz of the butter into small pieces and place in the well with the egg yolk, water and salt.

Work the butter, yolk, water and salt together with the fingertips and then draw in the flour, little by little. Knead lightly then wrap and chill for at least an hour.

Clean the leeks and cut into 2.5cm/1in chunks. Peel and trim the shallots. Place in a large covered pan with the oil. Cook over a low heat, shaking the pan from time to time until the vegetables are just tender. Cool and drain well, reserving any cooking liquor for the sauce.

Melt the remaining butter with the sugar in a 20cm/8in ovenproof skillet, if you have one. Otherwise, melt them together in a small saucepan and have ready a lined loose-bottomed cake tin. Allow the butter and sugar to bubble and darken slightly. If you are using a cake tin, pour the caramel mixture into the base of the tin, otherwise ensure that it is evenly spread over the base of the skillet.

Arrange the leeks and shallots neatly over the sugar mixture. Season well with salt and pepper. Scatter over the cheese cut in slivers.

Roll out the pastry quite thinly (you will have a fair amount left over). Cut into a round to fit the skillet or tin and lay it over the cheese, tucking the edges in.

Bake at 220°C/425°F/gas mark 7 for 25–30 minutes until golden brown. Invert onto a warmed plate (watch out for hot juices) and serve.

Bramble Sauce

3 shallots, finely chopped
1 large knob of butter
1 cinnamon stick
4 allspice berries
4 black peppercorns
1 small dried red chilli pepper
250g/8oz blackberries
200ml/7fl oz red wine (soft ripe Bergerac would be fine)
the juices from the leeks used for the tarte tatin
golden caster sugar

Soften then brown the shallots in the butter. When golden, add the spices and fry a minute longer before adding the blackberries, wine and leek juices. Simmer in a covered pan for 20 minutes.

Strain into a clean pan, pressing gently to extract all the juice but not puréeing the fruit. Check seasonings and add sugar to taste. Bring to the boil and reduce by half.

Shredded Kale

1 tbs toasted sesame oil
1 cm/½in peeled root ginger, finely grated
2 cloves of garlic, crushed
450g/1lb kale, shredded into thin strips

Heat the oil in a wok or large pan. Fry the ginger and garlic for a minute – but do not allow to burn or the flavour in the oil will be bitter.

Add the kale and cook stirring for a few minutes until just tender. (If the kale sticks during cooking, add a tablespoon of water.) Serve immediately.

Celeriac and Potato Rösti

2 large potatoes
1 medium celeriac
salt
pepper
nutmeg
25 g/1 oz melted butter or 2 tbs olive oil

Thinly peel the potatoes and celeriac. Halve the potatoes and quarter the celeriac.

Parboil for 5 minutes then drain and coarsely grate into a large bowl. Season well with salt, pepper and freshly grated nutmeg. Drizzle over the butter or oil and combine with a fork as if dressing a salad.

To cook, heat a greased heavy frying pan. Add the grated potato and celeriac. Stir carefully, so as to avoid crushing the rösti but still allowing it to brown. This will take about 15 minutes over a moderate heat.

Chocolate Feuilletés with Café au Lait Cream

50g/2oz shelled hazelnuts
150g/6oz plain chocolate
100g/4oz good quality white chocolate
(cheaper brands do not melt successfully)
284ml/½ pt double cream
1 tbs strong coffee or a miniature of Kahlua (Mexican coffee liqueur)
12 physalis (Cape gooseberries)
icing sugar, to decorate

Place the hazelnuts under a low grill and toast until lightly browned. Shake the grill pan from time to time during cooking to ensure the nuts colour evenly. Tip them into a clean tea towel and rub away any brown skins. Allow to cool, then chop roughly.

Melt the plain chocolate in a bowl over hot water. Pour onto a silicon paper-lined baking tray and spread out to an oblong, 30 × 18cm/12 × 7½in. Keep the edges straight and the chocolate as even as possible. Sprinkle the chopped hazelnuts all over the chocolate. Leave the tray in a cool place until the chocolate is firm but not hard.

With a sharp knife, cut the chocolate into 18 rectangles, each 6 × 5cm/2½ × 2in.

Melt the white chocolate, then allow it to cool slightly. Whip the cream until just beginning to mound. Carefully stir in the white chocolate and the coffee or Kahlua.

To serve: lay a dark chocolate slice on each plate, top with a spoon of the white chocolate cream and another rectangle of dark chocolate. Repeat, so that you have three leaves of dark chocolate and two layers of cream altogether.

Pull the papery physalis pods apart to expose the fruit. Bend the casings back up the stems and twist to give a jaunty topknot. Lay a couple on each plate and dust with the merest hint of icing sugar. Serve with small cups of Kahlua-spiked black coffee.

Menu for September

II

Fresh Figs with White Stilton Pâté

Spiced Brochettes with
Plum Sauce and Couscous

Kiwi Clafoutis

Menu for September
II

This menu is very simple to put together. Bulgar wheat, rice or millet can be used instead of couscous.

Kiwi fruit are now grown in southern France and Italy and are being used increasingly in traditional puddings. Cherries are the original fruit but damsons, pears, even grapes are also good. If you haven't time to make the sauces, simply serve with a dribble of single cream.

SHOPPING LIST

Greengrocery
1 bulb garlic
2 shallots
garlic chives
1 lemon
1 small ripe pineapple
2 unripe bananas
450 g/1 lb plums
10 kiwi fruits
an unwaxed lime
250 g/8 oz blackberries
6 large fresh figs
6 large vine leaves if available – if not use feuilles de chênes lettuce
fresh coriander leaves or mint leaves
3 very long, large sweet red peppers
225 g/8 oz pickling onions
225 g/8 oz small chestnut mushrooms
225 g/8 oz courgettes
225 g/8 oz cherry tomatoes

Dairy
225 g/8 oz white Stilton
150 g/5 oz butter
300 ml/½ pt single cream
5 eggs

Grocery
30 g/1 oz walnuts
450 g/1 lb couscous
raspberry vinegar – use balsamic if unavailable
lemon vinegar
heather honey
clear honey
shoyu soy sauce
mild curry powder
dried red chilli
cumin seeds
ground cinnamon
sesame oil
flour
demerara sugar
caster sugar
icing sugar to taste
sugar
½ bottle white port
miniature of Crème des Mûres

SUGGESTED ACTION PLAN

1   Make Stilton pâté.
2   Assemble brochettes – leave to marinate.
3   Put couscous to soak.
4   Make fruit purées and plum sauce.
5   Make clafoutis.
6   Steam couscous.
7   Fill figs.
8   Grill brochettes, reheat sauce.

Fresh Figs with White Stilton Pâté

225 g/8 oz white Stilton
a small bunch of garlic chives
30 g/1 oz walnuts
75 ml/2½ fl oz white port
6 large fresh figs
6 large vine leaves if available – if not use feuilles de chênes lettuce
2 tsp raspberry vinegar – use balsamic if unavailable
2 tbs heather honey

Finely grate the cheese. Chop the chives and walnuts. Mash the cheese, chives and walnuts with the port. Roll into balls the size of a large gobstopper. Leave in a cool place for a day.

To serve: cut a fig almost into four, pulling the points back to make a flower shape. Sit the fig on top of a vine or lettuce leaf. Place a cheese ball in the centre of each fig. Warm the raspberry vinegar with the honey and dribble over the cheese.

Spiced Brochettes

Brochettes
3 very long, large sweet red peppers
1 small ripe pineapple
225 g/8 oz pickling onions
225 g/8 oz small chestnut (brown-skinned) mushrooms (ordinary button will do if not available)
225 g/8 oz courgettes, with a diameter no greater than 2 cm/¾ in
2 greenish medium bananas
225 g/8 oz firm cherry tomatoes

Marinade
4 tbs lemon vinegar
2 tbs clear honey
2 tsp shoyu soy sauce
2 tsp good quality mild curry powder
2 cloves garlic
2 tsp toasted cumin seeds

Cut the peppers in half lengthways. Discard the seeds and any white pith. Cook, covered, in a little boiling water for five minutes. Drain and cool under running water.

Peel and cut the pineapple into 2.5 cm/1 in cubes. Peel the onions, wipe the mushrooms. Trim the courgettes and cut into slices, 2.5 cm/1 in thick. Peel the bananas, and slice them in the same way.

Cut the peppers into long ribbons about 2 cm/¾ in wide. Take a bamboo skewer and pierce a mushroom, through the stalk. Push it down to the base of the stick. Next thread the bottom of a pepper ribbon, without pushing it down, then thread a chunk of pineapple. Bend the pepper over the pineapple and push it onto the skewer again. Continue like this, snaking the pepper ribbons between each fruit or vegetable, all the way up the bamboo. Impale the banana, courgette and onion *crosswise* to ensure they do not drop off under the grill. Fill your skewers in whichever order you prefer, then lay them in a large flat dish.

Combine the lemon vinegar, honey, soy sauce and curry powder in a small saucepan. Add the very finely chopped garlic and cumin seeds and warm gently. Brush all over the brochettes and allow to stand for an hour.

Grill, turning occasionally, until the onions are tender. Serve with plum sauce and couscous.

Plum Sauce

2 shallots
2 cloves garlic
1 tsp sesame oil
1 dried red chilli
450g/1 lb Victoria plums – alternatively very dark plums can be used
150ml/5 fl oz water
a little sugar
salt
pepper

Finely chop the shallots and garlic and toss in a pan with the sesame oil. Cook very slowly, in a lidded pan, until softened. Add the chilli, the stoned plums and the water. Simmer until soft and thick. Pass through a sieve into a clean pan and balance seasonings, adding sugar, salt and pepper to taste. Serve hot. Reheat with a knob of butter if liked.

Couscous

450g/1 lb couscous
½ tsp salt
water
125 g/4 oz butter
1 lemon
1 tsp ground cinnamon
fresh coriander leaves or mint leaves

Place the couscous in a large flat dish. Sprinkle it well with salt. Pour on enough boiling water to cover then pour it off again. Allow the couscous to stand 15 minutes while it swells. Steam couscous in a strainer or colander over boiling water for 30 minutes, then put it into a warm dish.

Melt the butter with a few drops of lemon juice. Pour the butter over the couscous. Sprinkle with the cinnamon and work lightly with two forks to get rid of any lumps, distribute the butter and fluff it up. Top with the coriander or mint leaves.

Kiwi Clafoutis

a knob of butter
3 tbs demerara sugar
10 kiwi fruits
an unwaxed lime
300ml/½pt single cream
125g/4oz caster sugar
5 eggs
50g/2oz flour
250g/8oz blackberries
2 tbs Crème des Mûres
icing sugar to taste

Butter 6 individual flat gratin dishes. Sprinkle them with the demerara sugar.

Peel the kiwis. Cut 6 into quarters lengthwise and purée the other 4. Grate all the zest from the lime and place it in a large mixing bowl. Squeeze the juice and add it to the kiwi purée. Chill.

Add the cream, caster sugar, eggs and flour to the zest and, with a large whisk, beat to a smooth cream. Pour the batter into the prepared dishes. Drop in the kiwi quarters and bake at 190°C/375°F/gas mark 5 for 25 minutes.

Sieve the blackberries and stir in the Crème des Mûres. Add icing sugar to taste – you may not want any.

To serve: place a puddle of the blackberry sauce on one side of the plate and a puddle of the kiwi on the other. Tap and jiggle the plate until the two just meet – do not mix. Place a warm clafoutis on top and serve.

If preferred, the clafoutis can be baked in one large dish.

Menu for October

I

SALADE CREOLE

PUMPKIN RISOTTO
GARLIC CORNSTICKS
THREE TOMATO SALSA

PLUM DUMPLINGS AND CINNAMON CREAM

Menu for October

I

The contrasts of autumn weather are reflected in this menu: warm sunny days can follow frosty or misty nights. The Mauritian-influenced salad precedes the warming, creamy risotto. Pumpkins come in all shapes and sizes these days. Ideally for this dish, small round orangey-golden ones are required. They will be more plentiful towards the end of the month when thoughts turn to Hallowe'en.

One large plum pie can be made in much less time – simply line a baking tray with a few buttered filo sheets, cover with the stoned plums, sprinkle with half the sugar, cinnamon and crumbs and cover with more filo. Bake until crisp and brown and cut into wedges to serve.

SHOPPING LIST

Greengrocery
1 large Spanish onion
root ginger
1 bulb garlic
1 large red pepper
1–2 plantains
a cos lettuce
1 lime
6 baby pumpkins – about 12.5 cm/5 in diameter *or* a medium-sized pumpkin
3 large red onions
2 small green (unripe) tomatoes
18 dark plums
1 orange
a large sprig of rosemary
marjoram or oregano

2 chillies
chives
a small bunch of coriander *or* flat-leaved parsley

Dairy
3 eggs
125 g/4 oz Gorgonzola
100 g/3 oz Parmesan
170 g/6 oz butter or vegetable margarine
125 g/4 oz unsalted butter
284 ml/½ pt double cream
275 ml/½ pt buttermilk or milk

Grocery
sunflower or corn oil + some for frying
olive oil
3 sun-dried tomato halves (preferably the sort preserved in oil)
nutmeg
cayenne
mild curry powder
celery salt
ground cinnamon
a stick of cinnamon bark
1 large tin hearts of palm
450 g/1 lb arborio rice
150 ml/5 fl oz Marsala
1 lt/1¾ pt vegetable stock or water
100 g/3 oz pine kernels
bread
cornmeal – do not use 'instant' polenta
self-raising flour
soft brown sugar
demerara sugar
honey
red wine or balsamic vinegar
18 sheets of filo pastry

SUGGESTED ACTION PLAN

1   Make the cornsticks.
2   Prepare the first stage of the salad.
3   Fry the plantains.
4   Make the salsa.
5   Make the plum dumplings.
6   Finish the salad.
7   Hollow out the pumpkins and make the risotto.
8   Serve salad.
9   Grill top of pumpkins, reheat the cornsticks, heat the cream.

Salade Creole

1 large Spanish onion
1 cm/½in piece fresh root ginger
3 cloves garlic
1 large red pepper
2 tbs sunflower or corn oil + some for frying
salt
pepper
cayenne
1–2 plantains
1 tsp mild curry powder
1 large tin hearts of palm
a cos lettuce
1 lime
a small bunch of coriander or flat-leaved parsley

Finely chop the onion, grate the ginger and crush the garlic. Deseed the pepper, removing any membranes, and thinly slice. Place all the prepared vegetables in a pan with the 2 tbs oil and cook gently for 10 minutes, stirring occasionally. Season well with salt, pepper and cayenne. Cool then chill.

Peel then slice the plantains. Drop into hot oil and fry until crisp. Drain then shake in a paper bag with the curry powder to dust.

Drain the hearts of palm and then cut into thin rounds. Wash the lettuce and use to line 6 individual or one large salad plate. Spread the hearts of palm over the lettuce and top with the cooked vegetables. Thinly slice the lime and place around the edge of the salad(s) alternately with the plantains. Sprinkle with the chopped coriander or parsley.

Pumpkin Risotto

6 baby pumpkins – about 12.5 cm/5 in diameter
or a medium-sized pumpkin
3 large red onions
4 cloves of garlic
1 small chilli
4 tbs good olive oil
450 g/1 lb arborio rice
150 ml/5 fl oz Marsala
1 lt/1¾ pt vegetable stock or water
salt
black pepper
nutmeg
125 g/4 oz Gorgonzola
2 tbs chopped chives
100 g/3 oz Parmesan
100 g/3 oz pine kernels
2 tbs breadcrumbs

Cut the top off the pumpkin(s) and scoop out the insides. Save the empty shell(s). Roast the seeds if liked with tamari soy sauce as an appetizer. Discard any stringy bits. Chop the remaining flesh into tiny dice. Weigh out 285 g/10 oz and use the remainder for pie or whatever.

Heat the stock or water until barely simmering. Finely chop the red onion, garlic and deseeded chilli. Fry them gently until soft. Stir in the rice. Add the pumpkin and the Marsala. Cook until the wine is absorbed then add a ladleful of stock or water. Season very well with salt, black pepper and nutmeg. When the liquid is almost all absorbed, stir in another ladleful. Continue adding liquid as necessary until the rice is soft with just a tiny hard centre – this will take about 20 minutes but test it as you go along. If the rice is very absorbent and you run out of stock, use boiling water from the kettle. Stir in the Gorgonzola and chives. Grate the Parmesan and toss together with the pine kernels and breadcrumbs. Fill the pumpkin shell(s) with the risotto. Top with the Parmesan/pine kernels. Flash under the grill and serve.

Garlic Cornsticks

170 g/6 oz butter or vegetable margarine
275 ml/½ pt buttermilk or milk
a large sprig of rosemary
3 eggs
4 cloves garlic
1 green chilli
oil
340 g/12 oz cornmeal
170 g/6 oz self-raising flour
1 tsp celery salt
2 tbs soft brown sugar
black pepper

Put the butter, milk and rosemary into a pan over a low heat until the butter has completely melted. Do not allow to boil. Cool completely. Remove the rosemary. Add the eggs and lightly whisk. Finely chop the garlic and the seeded chilli and stir into the milk.

Pour a little oil into corn pone trays or use boudoir biscuit or Yorkshire pudding tins. Put in a hot oven 200°C/400°F/gas mark 6. Sift the cornmeal with the flour, celery salt, sugar and plenty of freshly ground black pepper. Stir in the milk, combining with brisk, light strokes – DO NOT BEAT.

Spoon the batter into the hot tins, do not overfill. Bake for 25 minutes. Loosen and turn out onto a rack to cool. Reheat loosely wrapped in foil.

Three Tomato Salsa

2 small green (unripe) tomatoes
salt
450g/1lb very ripe flavoursome tomatoes (smell before you buy)
1–2 cloves garlic according to taste
3 sun-dried tomato halves (preferably the sort preserved in oil)
1 tbs chopped marjoram or oregano
3 tbs olive oil
1 tbs red wine or balsamic vinegar
pepper
brown sugar

Chop the green tomatoes into tiny dice. Sprinkle with salt and leave to drain. Scald and skin the ripe tomatoes. Chop well, discarding the seeds. (If you are in a hurry or you prefer, leave in the skin and seeds.) Place in a bowl and stir in the crushed garlic. Finely shred the sun-dried tomatoes and add to the ripe tomatoes with the herbs. Rinse the green tomatoes and add to the mixture. Stir in the oil and vinegar. Season to taste with more salt, pepper and brown sugar. Combine well.

Plum Dumplings and Cinnamon Cream

18 dark plums
125 g/4 oz unsalted butter
1 tbs ground cinnamon
60 g/2 oz breadcrumbs
60 g/2 oz demerara sugar
18 sheets of filo pastry approx 30 × 45 cm/12 × 18 in

Cream
284 ml/½ pt double cream
2 tbs honey
a small piece of orange peel
a stick of cinnamon bark

Stone the plums. Melt the butter. Combine the cinnamon, breadcrumbs and demerara together. Unwrap the filo and place under a clean, damp tea towel. Take one sheet and place the narrow end facing you. Brush it with butter. Sprinkle it lightly with the spice mixture. Fold it in half, top to bottom. Turn the filo around by 90°. Brush and sprinkle it again. Place a plum in the middle of the bottom edge. Fold the pastry sides in to cover the plum. Brush with butter and roll up. Place on a baking tray. Repeat with the remaining filo and plums. Brush all the finished filo pastries with butter. Sprinkle with any remaining spice mixture and bake at 220°C/425°F/gas mark 7 for 15 minutes or until crisp and golden. Serve warm with cinnamon cream.

Combine the cream, honey, orange peel and cinnamon in a double boiler. Heat until steaming and allow to infuse. Strain and serve warm.

Menu for October

II

Wild Mushroom Ravioli in a Clear Broth

Red Cabbage Parcels
Carrot and Parsnip Cakes
Roast Apples

Muscat Pears with Spiced Crème Anglaise

Menu for October
II

There are bold clear flavours in this October menu. If you can go gathering your own mushrooms, so much the better. Many of the Forest Enterprises (set up by the Forestry Commission) now run autumn fungus forays. The French and Italians are very keen on mushroom hunting and after the first cool days of autumn can be seen exiting the towns by the carload to search in fields and woods. Some farmers put up large notices forbidding 'ramassage des champignons'. Local pharmacy windows are full of information on which mushrooms are good, and you can always pop in to check on your basketful. Failing such gentle pursuits, the bigger supermarkets and good greengrocers should be able to get you a selection of wild mushrooms.

I cannot remember who told me about Cassis and cabbage – it was not of my own devising – but whoever it was should be congratulated, they complement each other so well.

SHOPPING LIST

Greengrocery
450g/1lb fresh chestnuts
1 medium red cabbage
1 bulb oak-smoked garlic
1 bulb garlic
1 shallot
450g/1lb big carrots
340g/12oz parsnips
225g/8oz mixed mushrooms
750g/1½lb strong onions
a head of celery

6 firm, unripe Doyenné du Comice pears
6 small Cox's apples
elderberries – optional
thyme
sage
parsley
rosemary
bay

Dairy
5 eggs
284 ml/½ pt double cream
6 tsp Mascarpone
60 g/2 oz butter

Grocery
strong fine flour – Italian '00'
self-raising flour
golden caster sugar
caster sugar
a couple of dried mushrooms *or* a few drops of truffle oil – optional
oil
juniper berries
cardamom pods
ground cinnamon
1 stick of cinnamon
raisins
Amaretti – Italian bitter almond macaroons
candied citron peel
hazelnuts
Muscat raisins
½ bottle Muscat de Frontignan
½ bottle Crème de Cassis
½ bottle Pineau de Charente

SUGGESTED ACTION PLAN

1 Make carrot and parsnip cakes (this can be done well in advance).
2 Make broth.
3 Make pasta dough.
4 Make cabbage parcels.
5 Prepare pears, infuse cream.
6 Make ravioli.
7 Roast apples.
8 Make custard, reduce syrup.
9 Poach ravioli, serve.
10 Fry carrot and parsnip cakes immediately before serving.

Wild Mushroom Ravioli in a Clear Broth

Ravioli
125 g/4 oz strong fine flour – Italian '00'
1 egg + 1 yolk
a couple of dried mushrooms or a few drops of truffle oil – optional
salt
2 cloves garlic
1 shallot
30 g/1 oz butter
225 g/8 oz mixed mushrooms
6 tsp Mascarpone

Broth
450 g/1 lb strong onions
3 cloves garlic
2 large old carrots
a head of celery
2 tbs oil
150 ml/5 fl oz Pineau de Charente
1 lt/1¾ pt water
a bouquet of herbs to include thyme, sage, parsley, rosemary and bay
salt
pepper

Knead together the flour, egg, extra yolk and a good pinch of salt, incorporating the finely ground dried mushrooms or the truffle oil, if using. Keep kneading for 10 minutes or so, until the dough is smooth and elastic. Wrap and leave to rest.

Finely chop the garlic and shallot. Sauté slowly in the butter. Chop the cleaned mushrooms and add to the softened shallot. Cook until tender. Drain, reserving the pan juices.

Roughly chop the broth vegetables, there is no need to remove all the onion peel – a little will add colour. Fry briskly in the oil until colouring. Pour in the Pineau de Charente. Boil off then add the water and herbs. Season well. Simmer for 45 minutes then strain through a muslin-lined sieve. Add the pan juices to the broth. Check seasoning.

Roll out the dough until very thin, you should be able to read through it. Stamp out 12 × 7.5 cm/3 in circles. Place a good spoonful of the prepared mushroom mixture and a teaspoon of Mascarpone on six of the pasta rounds. Damp the edges, cover with another round and seal by pinching tightly all the way around. Poach in the broth for 3–4 minutes. Serve in flat soup plates – one ravioli per person.

Red Cabbage Parcels

450g/1 lb fresh chestnuts
1 medium red cabbage
2 onions
3 cloves oak-smoked garlic
3 tbs oil
2 juniper berries
1 stick of cinnamon
60 g/2 oz raisins
200ml/7 fl oz Crème de Cassis

Score the chestnuts and place them in a hot oven for ten minutes. Peel and chop them. Reserve 6 large, perfect leaves from the cabbage and finely chop the rest. Blanch or steam the leaves for 2 minutes.

Chop the onions and garlic and fry in the oil with the juniper berries and cinnamon. Allow to get golden brown then add the chestnuts, cabbage and raisins. Cook over a moderate heat for 10 minutes, stirring from time to time. Discard the cinnamon.

Lightly grease a baking dish. Fill the reserved leaves with the mixture, tucking up neatly to make parcels. Place in the dish and pour over the Crème de Cassis. Cover tightly and bake at 180°C/350°F/gas mark 4 for 1 hour. Serve the parcels, standing on a carrot and parsnip cake, dribbled with the cooking liquor.

Carrot and Parsnip Cakes

340g/12oz big carrots
340g/12oz parsnips
a big knob of butter
salt
about 175g/6oz self-raising flour

Peel the carrots and parsnips and cook until tender. Mash well with the butter and season with salt. Cool. Turn onto a floured board and work in the flour, kneading well. Roll out to slightly less than 1cm/½in thickness and cut into 6 neat squares.

Pre-heat a griddle or heavy frying pan. Do not add any fat. Cook about 3–4 minutes a side until nicely browned. These cakes can be made in advance and reheated as necessary.

Roast Apples

6 small Cox's apples
oil
elderberries – optional
6–12 fresh sage leaves

Run a thick film of oil around a roasting tin and place it in a hot oven – 220°C/425°F/gas mark 7. With a sharp knife score around the middle of the apples. Place in the hot oil. Roast for 15 minutes or until browned and soft.

If using elderberries, destalk them and pop briefly in a pan with a little sugar. When the apples are cooked, scoop out the core and fill with a teaspoonful of elderberries.

Serve each apple with a leaf or two of sage.

Port, Stilton and Walnut Christmas Wreath, with Rosemary Roast Potatoes, Parsnip Quenelles and Brussels Sprouts with Mustard Cream (December I: see pp.207-10)

Brandied Mushroom Parfait with Truffled Sauce (December II: see p.217)

Muscat Pears
with Spiced Crème Anglaise

Pears
60 g/2 oz Amaretti – Italian bitter almond macaroons
25 g/1 oz candied citron peel
25 g/1 oz Muscat raisins
60 g/2 oz toasted grated hazelnuts
1 egg white
6 firm, unripe Doyenné du Comice pears
½ bottle Muscat de Frontignan
50 g/2 oz golden caster sugar

Crème Anglaise
4–6 cardamom pods
a pinch of ground cinnamon
284 ml/½ pt double cream
60 g/2 oz caster sugar
3 egg yolks

Crush the Amaretti and chop the peel and raisins finely. Combine with the hazelnuts and enough egg white to make a paste.

Peel the pears, retaining the stalks and keeping whole. Using a small Parisien baller or potato peeler remove the core through the base of each pear. Fill the cavity with Amaretti/nut mixture. Place upright in a deep lidded casserole dish. Pour over the wine. Cover and cook in a slow oven, basting occasionally if necessary, until tender.

While the pears are cooking, place the cream in the top of a double boiler with the crushed cardamom seeds and ground cinnamon and warm gently. Allow to infuse. Lightly beat the egg yolks with the caster sugar and strain on the hot cream. Return to the double boiler and cook, stirring until the mixture coats the back of the spoon.

Remove pears and keep warm. Strain the liquor into a clean pan. Add the golden caster sugar and warm gently until dissolved. Bring to the boil and reduce until syrupy.

To serve: stand a pear on a hot plate, pour over the Muscat syrup. Dribble the strained spiced custard around the bottom, feathering it into the syrup puddle if desired.

Menu for November

I

GRILLED CROTTINS WITH RED ONION MARMALADE
AND ROCKET

CRÊPES DE CHINE
COCONUT RICE
PICKLES

ALMOND CHOCOLATE MARQUISE
WITH KUMQUATS

Menu for November
I

Goat's cheese used to be purely seasonal, available in the spring and summer. Now we can get it all year around. Ordinary cooking onions can be used instead of the red ones but it would be a shame to lose the colour.

The spring rolls, Crêpes de Chine, are deliberately light to balance the exceptionally rich marquise. This recipe came out of several I know. I don't think there is a more unctuous pudding – I do recommend the sharpness of the kumquats to go with it. Both the marquise and kumquats should be prepared the day before.

SHOPPING LIST

Greengrocery
450 g/1 lb red onions
1 bunch spring onions
1 bulb garlic
ginger root
225 g/8 oz carrots
225 g/8 oz celeriac
125 g/4 oz mangetouts
1 small red pepper
125 g/4 oz white cabbage
300 g/10 oz mooli
1 lime
4 medium tomatoes
1 large chilli
rocket leaves
125 g/4 oz kumquats

Dairy
2 eggs
6 crottins chavignol goat's cheese
100 g/3½ oz unsalted butter
568 ml/1 pt double cream

Grocery

sesame oil
oil
balsamic vinegar
tamari soy sauce
soft brown sugar
caster sugar
dark rye bread
olive oil
12 spring roll skins
125 g/4 oz tofu
cocoa powder

1 cinnamon stick
arrowroot
dry sherry
jasmine rice
400 g/14 oz tin coconut milk
star anise
125 g/4 oz shelled and blanched almonds
125 g/4 oz plain chocolate
coffee
½ bottle sweet Marsala
miniature of Grand Marnier or Cointreau

SUGGESTED ACTION PLAN

1   Prepare the marquise and kumquats the previous day.
2   Make the filling for the crêpes.
3   Prepare the onion marmalade.
4   Make the pickles.
5   Roll up the crêpes.
6   Cook the rice.
7   Fry the pancakes.
8   Grill the crottins.

Grilled Crottins with Red Onion Marmalade and Rocket

450g/1 lb red onions
1 tbs sesame oil
1 tbs balsamic vinegar
100g/3½oz soft brown sugar
6 slices of dark rye bread
6 crottins chavignol goat's cheese
a good handful of rocket leaves
olive oil

Very finely slice the onions and place them in a heavy-bottomed pan with the sesame oil. Cover and cook very slowly until soft. Add the vinegar and sugar. Stir until sugar is dissolved then cook until thick. Serve just warm.

Toast one side of the bread. Turn over. Place one crottin on each slice of bread and put back under the grill until the cheese is lightly browned and bubbling. Trim any over-browned bits of toast and serve wreathed with the rocket, dribbled with the oil and accompanied by the onion marmalade.

Crêpes de Chine

125 g/4 oz tofu
sesame oil
2 tsp tamari soy sauce
1 bunch spring onions
2 cloves garlic
1 cm/½ in fresh root ginger
225 g/8 oz carrots
225 g/8 oz celeriac
125 g/4 oz mangetouts
1 small red pepper
125 g/4 oz white cabbage
2 tsp arrowroot
2 tbs dry sherry
1 egg white
12 spring roll skins
oil

Cut the tofu into thin strips and fry quickly in hot sesame oil. Drain and pour over the tamari soy sauce. Leave to cool.

Shred all the vegetables and cook in a large pan or wok in a little sesame oil for 3 minutes. Stir in the tofu. Slake 1 tsp of arrowroot with the sherry. Stir into the vegetables and cook 1 minute longer. Cool.

Make a paste with the remaining teaspoon of arrowroot and the egg white.

Spread out one spring roll skin with a corner towards you (to make a diamond shape). Place a good spoonful (¹⁄₁₂) of the mixture on the skin, about 5 cm/2 in up. Fold the diamond point over the filling and the sides in. Dab with the arrowroot and roll up. Dab the final point with arrowroot to seal. Repeat with the remaining skins and mixture. Fry in deep oil until crisp – about 10 minutes – and serve with the rice and pickles.

Coconut Rice

300g/10oz jasmine rice
400ml/14oz tinned coconut milk
8 star anise
salt

Wash the rice and drain well. Place it in a heavy-bottomed pan that has a close fitting lid. Add the coconut milk, 2 star anise, and a good pinch of salt. Stir then bring to the boil. Simmer, uncovered, until the coconut milk has been completely absorbed (about 10 minutes), then cover tightly and cook over minimum heat for a further 10 minutes. Mould quickly into individual pyramids – either with your hands or by using a lightly oiled cup – and top each with a star anise.

Pickles

300g/10oz mooli
2tsp salt
1 lime
4 medium tomatoes
1 large chilli
1tsp brown sugar
1tsp tamari soy sauce

Coarsely grate the mooli and place it in a sieve. Pour over boiling water and drain well. Combine with the salt and leave to stand in the sieve with a weight on for 2 hours. Using a zester make fine curls of the lime peel and mix with the mooli. Squeeze a few drops of lime juice onto the mooli, mix and serve.

Scald the tomatoes and skin. Remove the seeds from the chilli. Chop both finely and cook over a low heat for 5 minutes. Purée and push through a sieve. Mix in the sugar and soy whilst still warm then chill before serving.

Almond Chocolate Marquise

125g/4oz shelled and blanched almonds
125g/4oz very dark chocolate (eg Green & Black's)
2tsp very strong black coffee
2tbs sweet Marsala
100g/3½oz unsalted butter
50g/2oz light brown sugar
1tbs cocoa powder
2 egg yolks
50g/2oz caster sugar
568ml/1pt double cream

Line 6 ramekins with cut-to-fit silicone paper or cling film. Arrange a 'flower' or 'star' of almonds in the base of each dish. Melt the chocolate, coffee and Marsala together in a bowl over hot water. Allow to cool a little. Beat the butter with the light brown sugar until light and fluffy. Fold in the cocoa. Whisk the egg yolks with the caster sugar until pale. Whip the cream. Beat the melted chocolate into the butter, then stir into the egg and fold in the cream. Divide between the prepared dishes. Chill for 12 hours. Turn out an hour before serving and allow to come to room temperature. Serve garnished with the poached kumquats.

Kumquats

125 g/4 oz caster sugar
125 ml/4 fl oz water
1 cinnamon stick
2 tbs Grand Marnier or Cointreau
125 g/4 oz kumquats

Mix the sugar and water together in a pan. Add the cinnamon stick and bring to the boil. Boil until syrupy and thick. Add the liqueur and the sliced kumquats and cook a further 3 minutes. Cool then chill.

Menu for November

II

La Garbure

Mushrooms en Chemise
Sweet Potato Mash
Cauliflower and Broccoli

Banana, Pecan and Maple Pudding

Menu for November
II

An appetite sharpened by brisk walks or wood stacking is required before tackling this menu. It is unashamedly hearty; it is peasanty comfort food for cold damp weather. *La Garbure* is a meal in itself in the Southwest of France. If your city slicker existence means you aren't up for it, serve a more delicate and refined vegetable soup instead.

SHOPPING LIST

Greengrocery
225 g/8 oz strong onions
125 g/4 oz shallots
2 bulbs garlic
2 leeks
225 g/8 oz carrots
1 head of celery
1 small white cabbage or savoy
225 g/8 oz fresh chestnuts
6 large flat mushrooms – approx 7.5 cm/3 in diameter
1 kg/2 lb sweet potatoes
1 large cauliflower
750 g/1½ lb broccoli
2 oranges
1 lemon
3–4 bananas
ginger root
sage
thyme

Dairy
2 egg yolks
150 g/6 oz butter
284 ml/½ pt double cream
60 ml/2 fl oz soured cream
225 g/8 oz Shropshire Blue

Grocery

225 g/8 oz haricot beans
90 g/3 oz shelled pecans
125 g/4 oz dried apricots
balsamic vinegar
olive oil
125 g/4 oz vegetable suet
maple syrup
plain flour
wholemeal flour – optional
baking powder

ground cinnamon
bay leaves
cloves
ground mace
cayenne
peppercorns
bread
3 vegetarian sausages – optional
12 sheets of filo pastry
½ bottle red wine

SUGGESTED ACTION PLAN

1 Soak beans.
2 Make pudding and apricot sauce.
3 Make soup.
4 Roast the chestnuts, prepare stuffed cabbage.
5 Grill the mushrooms.
6 Prepare the vegetables.
7 Finish mushrooms, make garlic and red wine sauce.
8 Cook sweet potatoes.
9 Put cabbage in soup, cook sausages.
10 Cook cauliflower and broccoli, serve soup.

La Garbure

225 g/8 oz haricot beans
2 tbs olive oil or butter
225 g/8 oz strong onions
3 cloves garlic
2 leeks
225 g/8 oz carrots
1 head of celery
1 lt/1¾ pt dark vegetable stock or water
bay leaf
1 tbs chopped sage
a few sprigs of thyme
4 cloves
6 crushed peppercorns
225 g/8 oz fresh chestnuts
125 g/4 oz breadcrumbs
2 egg yolks
½ tsp salt
pepper
ground mace
1 small white cabbage or savoy
3 vegetarian sausages – optional

Soak the beans for at least 1 hour. Chop the onion, garlic, leeks, carrots and celery. Braise for 5 minutes over a fairly high heat in the oil or butter. Add the haricot beans and the water or stock. Add the herbs and seasonings. Simmer for 1 hour.

Roast and peel the chestnuts. Chop finely and mix with the breadcrumbs. Moisten with a little of the soup. Mix to a stiff paste with the egg yolks. Season well with salt, pepper and a pinch of mace. Blanch six perfect leaves from the cabbage and fill each with the chestnut stuffing. Roll up, tucking the sides in. Shred the remaining cabbage. Put the cabbage and the cabbage rolls into the soup and cook a further 20 minutes.

If using the sausages, fry in a little oil, cut each into three and add to the soup, with the cooking fat, just before serving.

Serve with a good glass of gutsy red Côtes de Gascogne, pouring a little into each soup plate.

Mushrooms en Chemise

6 large flat mushrooms – approx 7.5 cm/3 in diameter
olive oil
2 tsp good balsamic vinegar
2 cloves of garlic
125 g/4 oz finely chopped shallots
1 tbs chopped sage
225 g/8 oz Shropshire Blue
12 sheets of filo pastry
30 g/1 oz melted butter

Sauce
15 g/½ oz butter
1 bulb garlic
375 ml/½ bottle red wine
peppercorns
bay leaf

Wipe the mushrooms and remove the stalks. Place cup side up in a flat heatproof dish. Drizzle with oil and the balsamic vinegar. Grill under a moderate heat for 10 minutes. Drain the mushrooms, reserving the juices for the sauce, and allow to cool.

Peel and chop the garlic and cook it slowly with the shallots in a little oil. Put the cooked garlic and shallots into a bowl with the sage and cubed Shropshire Blue. Combine well. Don't wash the pan – use it for sauce making.

Fill the mushrooms with the Shropshire Blue mixture. Brush one sheet of filo with the melted butter and lay another one on top. Place a mushroom, filled side down in the centre and brush the filo all around with more butter. Fold up neatly and place on a baking tray so the filled side (under the filo) is uppermost. Repeat with the rest of the filo and mushrooms. Bake at 330°C/425°F/gas mark 7 for 20–25 minutes until crisp and golden.

Peel the garlic cloves for the sauce and fry in the butter until just beginning to turn colour. Add the wine and mushroom juices. Flavour with the bay and peppercorns. Simmer for 15 minutes, then turn up the heat and reduce by half.

Sweet Potato Mash

1 kg/2 lb sweet potatoes – the orange-fleshed ones will look more attractive
5 cm/2 in piece root ginger
75 g/2½ oz butter
black pepper
salt
cayenne
1 orange – optional

Put a large pan of salted water on to boil. Put the peeled, bruised ginger into it. Boil the sweet potatoes in their skins until tender. Depending on size this will be about 30 minutes. Drain, reserving the cooking water and ginger.

Peel, then mash well with the butter. Finely chop a little of the cooked ginger and add it to the mash with freshly ground pepper and salt to taste. Pile up and dust the top with cayenne and some fine strips of orange zest.

Cauliflower and Broccoli

1 large cauliflower
750g/1½lb broccoli
butter
salt
pepper
60ml/2fl oz soured cream

Break the cauliflower and broccoli into florets – reserve any thick stalks for slicing and stir frying in another recipe. Thickly butter a heatproof soufflé dish or pudding basin. Pack the florets, heads down, neatly into the dish. Alternate broccoli and cauliflower and season as you go, building up the layers.

Place a steamer upside down over the filled dish and then invert. Do not remove the dish. Place the steamer over boiling water and cook for 15 minutes. Remove the steamer from the pan and stand on a folded tea towel, to dry the base, then invert. The cauliflower and broccoli will still be in their basin. Remove the steamer and invert the cauliflower and broccoli onto a serving dish. Top with the soured cream and another grinding of pepper.

Banana, Pecan and Maple Pudding

Pudding
250g/8oz plain flour – use half wholemeal if liked
2tsp baking powder
1tsp ground cinnamon
pinch of salt
125g/4oz vegetable suet
about 6tbs maple syrup
3–4 bananas, sliced
90g/3oz shelled pecans

Sauce
125g/4oz dried apricots – soaked in boiling water
1 orange
1 lemon
284ml/½pt double cream

Combine the flour, baking powder, cinnamon, salt and suet in a large bowl. Mix to a soft dough with a little water. Make three rounds of dough to fit into the pudding basin (7, 11 and 15cm/3, 4½ and 6in in diameter). Lay the smallest into the base of a well-greased basin. Drizzle over a little maple syrup (use a soft brown sugar if you've not got syrup), cover with a layer of bananas and nuts and add a little more syrup. Top with the next suet round and repeat the process using up the bananas, nuts and syrup. Lay the biggest suet circle on top, cover with greased paper and tie down. Steam for 2½ hours.

Simmer the apricots in a little water with the orange and lemon juice. When soft, purée and sieve.

To serve: turn out the pudding, and offer the apricot sauce and cream separately.

Menu for December

I

GUACAMOLE TURBANS

PORT, STILTON AND WALNUT CHRISTMAS WREATH
ROSEMARY ROAST POTATOES
PARSNIP QUENELLES
BRUSSELS SPROUTS WITH MUSTARD CREAM

CRANBERRY AND ORANGE COMPÔTE
WITH BROWN SUGAR MERINGUES

Menu for December
I

If I was using this menu or the next for my Christmas Day Dinner, I would also serve a traditional Christmas Pudding, in all its flaming glory, complete with brandy butter. As Christmas puds are made so far in advance there would be no need to alter the action plan to accommodate it.

SHOPPING LIST

Greengrocery
6 ripe avocados
1 bulb garlic
450g/1lb shallots or red onions
1 long leek
1 small head of celery
450g/1lb Brussels sprouts
125g/4oz chestnut mushrooms
18 small Desirée potatoes
450g/1lb parsnips
1 lemon
1 very large or 2 medium red peppers
1 very large or 2 medium green peppers
1 very large or 2 medium yellow peppers
3 sweet oranges
450g/1lb cranberries
coriander leaves
fresh or dried rosemary

Dairy
8 eggs
250ml/9fl oz crème fraîche
150g/6oz butter
200g/7oz Stilton
340g/12oz Mascarpone

Grocery
bread
olive oil
plain flour
100g/3½oz shelled walnuts
golden granulated sugar
golden caster sugar
caster sugar
dried chillies
allspice berries

pink peppercorns – optional
mustard seeds
nutmeg
ground cinnamon
1 large cinnamon stick
cloves
½ bottle ruby port
miniature of Crème de Cassis

SUGGESTED ACTION PLAN

1 Make meringues and compôte the day before.
2 Make choux puffs.
3 Roast peppers.
4 Cook parsnips.
5 Make Stilton filling.
6 Make turbans, toast or fry bread.
7 Make quenelles.
8 Make leek ribbons and glaze.
9 Prepare Brussels.
10 Fill puffs and heat wreath, bake quenelles.
11 Serve turbans.
12 Cook Brussels and glaze wreath.
13 Assemble meringues just before serving.

Guacamole Turbans

6 ripe avocados
2 large cloves garlic
1 lemon
olive oil
salt
pepper
1 very large or 2 medium red peppers
1 very large or 2 medium green peppers
1 very large or 2 medium yellow peppers
6 slices bread
some fresh coriander leaves

Purée the avocados with the garlic and the juice of half the lemon until fairly smooth. Beat in a tablespoon of olive oil. Season with salt and pepper.

Place the peppers under a hot grill until their skins blacken and blister. Peel away the papery skin and remove the seeds and stalks. Cut into 0.5 cm/¼ in strips. Lightly oil 6 individual pudding basins – use tea cups if you have none. Starting in the base of each basin, wind pepper strips round and round to cover the sides of the basin. Alternate the colours. Fill the centre with the avocado mixture, packing it well down and levelling the top. Keep in a cool place until ready to serve.

Cut the bread into rounds slightly larger than the top of your moulds and toast or fry them until golden. Place one round in the centre of each plate. With a round-bladed knife loosen the sides of the moulds and invert onto the toast. Dribble over a little really good olive oil and decorate with coriander leaves and a little lemon rind.

Port, Stilton and Walnut Christmas Wreath

Choux
250ml/9fl oz water
100g/3½oz butter
150g/5oz plain flour
½ tsp salt
4–5 eggs
100g/3½oz shelled walnuts, finely chopped
1 egg yolk
a pinch of salt

Filling
450g/1lb shallots or red onions
3 cloves garlic
1 small head celery
125g/4oz chestnut mushrooms
2tbs olive oil
300ml/½pt ruby port
200g/7oz Stilton
pepper
1 long leek
75g/2½oz golden granulated sugar
2 dried chillies
3 allspice berries
a few sprigs fresh or dried rosemary
a few pink peppercorns or just-cooked cranberries

Put the water into a pan and add the butter. Melt over a low heat but do not boil. Sift the flour and salt. Beat the whole eggs in a little bowl or jug. Tip the flour into the hot water and beat well over a low heat until a soft ball is formed and it leaves the sides of the pan cleanly. Take off the heat and begin to beat the egg in a little at a time. It may not absorb all the egg – if you have any left over you can save it for brushing the paste with before baking. Beat in the walnuts.

Pipe or spoon 3.5cm/1½in balls of paste onto a silicone paper-lined or greased baking sheet. Mix any of the remaining egg with the yolk and salt and lightly brush the very tops of the paste balls. Bake at 200°C/400°F/gas mark 6 for 20–25 minutes. Transfer to a cooling rack and slit the sides to allow the steam to escape.

Finely chop the onions, garlic, celery and mushrooms and cook in the oil until lightly browning. Pour in 3 tbs of the port. Cook slowly until soft then turn up the heat to boil off the liquid. Mix in the crumbled Stilton. Season with pepper.

Clean the leek and slice it lengthwise, from top to bottom. Poach it in the rest of the port (and a little water if necessary) until just tender. Remove from the pan and cool. Add the sugar to the pan with the dried chillies and allspice berries. Stir until the sugar dissolves then boil hard until syrupy.

Fill the puffs with the Stilton mixture. If you have a large heatproof platter, pile the puffs into a 25 cm/10 in ring – otherwise spread out on a baking sheet and set a serving platter to warm to assemble the puffs later. Reheat at 190°C/375°F/gas mark 5 for about 10 minutes.

Tie the leek strips into 3 or 5 bows. Have ready the puffs in their ring. Dribble over the port glaze. Decorate with the leek bows, rosemary sprigs and pink peppercorns or cranberries. Serve.

Rosemary Roast Potatoes

18 small (ping pong ball-sized) Desirée potatoes
2 tbs olive oil
a sprig of fresh rosemary or some dried
pepper
salt

S crub and dry the potatoes. Place in a cast-iron casserole or similar and dribble on the oil and add the seasoning. Turn the potatoes about. Cover tightly and put in a hot oven 200°C/400°F/gas mark 6 for 1 hour. Uncover and cook a further 15 minutes.

Parsnip Quenelles

450 g/1 lb parsnips
4 tbs crème fraîche
2 egg yolks
salt
nutmeg
15 g/½ oz butter

B oil the parsnips until tender then mash with the crème fraîche. Do not use anything more high tech than a potato masher or a fork – electric gadgets will ruin this dish. Beat in the egg yolks and season well with salt and freshly grated nutmeg.

Using two spoons or a piping bag form into neat 'robin's eggs'. Place in a greased dish and top with shavings of butter and a dusting of more nutmeg. Either brown under the grill to finish or cool and, when required, reheat in a hot oven 200°C/400°F/gas mark 6 until piping hot and nicely browned.

Brussels Sprouts with Mustard Cream

450g/1lb Brussels sprouts
2 tsp mustard seeds
30g/1oz butter
200ml/7fl oz crème fraîche

Shred the Brussels sprouts coarsely. Heat the mustard seeds in a pan until they begin to pop. Add the butter and when it has melted stir in the sprouts. Spoon over the cream. Lightly mix, cover and cook over a low heat for 7 minutes. Season well with salt and pepper before serving.

Cranberry and Orange Compôte
with Brown Sugar Meringues

3 egg whites
175 g/6 oz golden caster sugar
1 tsp ground cinnamon
3 sweet oranges
1 large cinnamon stick
3 cloves
4 allspice berries
150 ml/5 fl oz water
150 g/5 oz caster sugar
340 g/12 oz cranberries
2 tbs Crème de Cassis
340 g/12 oz Mascarpone

Whisk the egg whites until stiff then whisk in the golden caster sugar a little at a time until all is incorporated. Fold through the cinnamon. Don't mix too much. Swirls of the spice through the meringue are fine. Lightly oil a baking tray or line with silicone paper. Pipe 12 × 10 cm/4 in 5-pointed stars – try to make them all the same. An easy way to do this is to make a template with thick black lines, slip it under the baking paper and pipe over it, moving it along for each star. Bake at a minimum heat 110 C/225°F/gas mark ¼ for 2 hours. Cool slowly then keep in an airtight tin.

Peel a large swathe of zest from one of the oranges. Put it in a pan with the cinnamon stick, cloves, allspice berries, water and caster sugar. Warm gently until the sugar has dissolved then boil until syrupy. Leave to cool and infuse.

Wash the cranberries and simmer in a very little water until tender. Drain. Strain the syrup and add to the cranberries. Pare a few streamers of the orange zest and add to the cranberries. Peel the oranges, removing every scrap of pith. Quarter then slice and mix into the cranberries. Stir in the Cassis. Check the compôte and add a very little sugar if required but remember you are serving with meringues.

To serve: sandwich a pair of stars together with the Mascarpone. Fill so that the top (single) points meet but the bottom 'legs' are splayed out – so that the star pairs can stand upright. Surround with a couple of spoonfuls of compôte. Serve immediately or face collapse!

Menu for December

II

Brandied Mushroom Parfait with Truffled Sauce

Christmas en Croûte
Red Wine Sauce
Fondant Potatoes
Mixed Game Chips
Sautéed Savoy

Pastiche Gascon

Menu for December
II

Christmas is traditionally a time for being indulgent and how better than to treat everyone to the fabled black diamonds. Truffles become the star on the Christmas tree in a slightly frivolous but pretty starter.

I have used raised pies for Christmas before. Their Victorian style seems entirely appropriate, adding scale and focus to the festive table. This pie with its layers of red, white and green has so many Christmas flavours crammed under its lid. Do slice it at the table.

Throughout the Gers, instead of signs advertising cream teas as here, the ferme auberges offer 'foie gras, confit et le vrai Pastis Gascon'. Every pâtisserie has them for sale on Sundays. Every good housewife knows how to make one but they will only tell you mysteriously that you must learn over years and years. The recipes are closely guarded and the skill of making the very fine pastry is handed down from mother to daughter. This 'pastiche' is then a simplified but nonetheless delicious fake.

SHOPPING LIST

Greengrocery
225 g/8 oz shallots
450 g/1 lb red onions
1 bulb oak-smoked garlic
1 bulb garlic
450 g/1 lb chestnut mushrooms
1 kg/2 lb leeks
1 celery
3 small tomatoes
small red pepper

small yellow pepper
small green pepper
1 sweet potato
2 carrots
1 parsnip
2 small beetroots
6 large potatoes
1 small savoy cabbage
125 g/4 oz cranberries
450 g/1 lb Cox's or Reinette apples
1 lemon
sage

Dairy
325 g/11 oz butter (or 175 g/6 oz may be hard margarine for the croûte)
125 g/4 oz unsalted butter
568 ml/1 pt double cream
200 g/7 oz smoked Wensleydale
5 eggs

Grocery
1 black truffle
150 ml/5 fl oz vegetable stock
sunflower oil
olive oil
plain flour
Gelozone
redcurrant jelly
nutmeg
1 cinnamon stick
ground allspice
peppercorns
2 bay leaves
saffron
bread
225 g/8 oz dried chestnuts
125 g/4 oz pistachios

60 g/2 oz shelled walnuts
125 g/4 oz pruneaux d'Agen
8 filo pastry sheets
sugar
¼ bottle brandy
½ bottle of claret
½ bottle Armagnac

SUGGESTED ACTION PLAN

1 Make the parfait the night before and prepare all the fillings for the croûte.
2 Soak the prunes.
3 Make the hot water crust and fill the pie.
4 Make the sauces.
5 Do the potatoes and game chips.
6 Make the pastiche.
7 Prepare the cabbage, egg wash pie sides.
8 Assemble parfait and serve.
9 Cook cabbage and warm game chips whilst dishing main course.

Brandied Mushroom Parfait with Truffled Sauce

225 g/8 oz shallots
3 cloves garlic
25 g/1 oz butter
450 g/1 lb chestnut mushrooms
150 ml/5 fl oz brandy
3 egg yolks
salt
pepper
284 ml/½ pt double cream
1 black truffle
150 ml/5 fl oz good, clear, dark vegetable stock
½ tsp Gelozone
6 slices of toast
3 small tomatoes
small pieces of red, yellow and green grilled peppers

Finely chop the shallots and garlic. Brown lightly in the butter. Add the chopped mushrooms and brandy and simmer in a covered pan for 10 minutes. Drain, reserving the pan juices. Purée in a liquidiser or food processor. Beat in the egg yolks and cook over a low heat for a few minutes until thickened, but not scrambled. Season well with salt and pepper. Cool. Whip the cream until it mounds then fold through the mushroom purée. Pile into a silicone paper-lined tin, preferably a deep V-shaped one. Smooth down and chill well overnight.

Peel the truffle, reserving the peelings, and cut into 6 slices. Cut each slice into a little star. Chop the truffle trimmings very finely. Warm the stock with the truffle peelings and allow to infuse. Whisk the Gelozone into the reserved pan juices. When dissolved, strain on the vegetable stock and add the finely chopped truffle trimmings. Heat until steaming. Pour a little truffle sauce into the base of each plate, cool until setting. Cut the toast into Christmas tree-shaped triangles and cover with the parfait, neatening the edges. Place the triangle on top of the sauce. Use a trimmed half of tomato as the Christmas tree 'pot' and decorate with the truffle star and tiny pieces of pepper. Serve.

Christmas en Croûte

225g/8oz dried chestnuts
½ bottle claret
1 bay leaf
450g/1lb red onions
olive oil
1 tbs finely chopped sage
black pepper
salt
1 small head white (forced) celery
nutmeg
200g/7oz smoked Wensleydale
2 eggs
1kg/2lb leeks
2 cloves garlic
175g/6oz butter or vegetable margarine
(the block variety is better e.g. 'Tomor')
175ml/6½fl oz water
450g/1lb plain flour
125g/4oz cranberries
ground allspice
125g/4oz pistachios

Soak the dried chestnuts, then cook slowly in all but 2tbs of the claret with a bay leaf. Cool and drain when tender – save the wine for sauce making. Roughly chop.

Finely chop the red onion and cook very slowly in 1tbs oil. When meltingly soft, add the reserved 2tbs of claret and sage. When the wine has reduced away, stir in the chestnuts, take off heat and season well with salt and pepper. Allow to cool.

Chop the celery and cook it slowly in a tablespoon of oil until softened. Season with freshly grated nutmeg and black pepper, stir in the crumbled Wensleydale. Mix in 1 egg.

Wash the leeks and leave in as long lengths as possible. Braise in a little oil with the sliced garlic, drain and cool when soft.

Lightly oil the base and sides of a loose-sided 1kg/2lb loaf tin or a game pie mould. Melt the butter or margarine with the water. Sift the flour with 1tsp salt. Make a well in the middle and pour in the hot water and fat. Work quickly to bring all together, kneading lightly. The dough should be soft like well-handled playdough. Use a little over two-thirds to line the tin, pressing well into the sides and bottom and leaving a 1cm/½in edge hanging over the sides of the tin. Avoid too much thickness at the corners. Beat the remaining egg with a teaspoon of water and brush over the inside. Keep the rest of the dough warm and covered.

Place the chestnuts over the base, sprinkle over the cranberries. Dust the cranberries with some ground allspice, cover with the leeks and scatter over the pistachios. Finally spread on the Wensleydale and celery. Lightly press down each layer as you go. The filling should stand proud of the tin.

Roll or press out the remaining dough and cover the pie, sealing the edges with the egg wash. Crimp boldly. Decorate with stars or leaves or even poinsettias (if you're feeling artistic) made out of the trimmings. Brush the top of the pie with the egg wash. Put in a moderately hot oven 200°C/400°F/gas mark 6 for 1 hour. Remove from the tin, brush the top and sides with egg and return to the oven for another 15 minutes.

Red Wine Sauce

a small jar redcurrant jelly – preferably home-made
but if unavailable the best quality you can buy
the wine the chestnuts were cooked in made up to 284ml/½pt
with good stock
1 cinnamon stick
a few peppercorns
a bay leaf

Place everything in a pan together. Heat slowly until the jelly melts then boil and reduce by a third. Check seasoning. Strain and serve.

Fondant Potatoes

6 large potatoes
125g/4oz butter
150ml/5fl oz water
a good pinch of saffron

Peel the potatoes and cut into 1.5cm/¾in thick slices. Cut the slices into neat shapes – stars are very pretty for a Christmas table but you can simply use hexagons or circles. Melt the butter in a roasting tin and add the water and saffron. Cover with greaseproof paper and cook until the water has boiled off and the potatoes are tender – about 30 minutes at 200°C/400°F/gas mark 6. Serve.

Mixed Game Chips

1 sweet potato
2 carrots
1 parsnip
2 small beetroots
1 lemon
sunflower oil
salt

Scrub the vegetables and slice on a mandolin. Drop all the slices except the beetroot into a large bowl of iced water containing the juice of the lemon. After 15 minutes drain and dry. Heat the oil until it is hot enough to brown a cube of bread in a little under 1 minute (190°C/375°F). Rinse and dry the beetroot slices very well. Fry the vegetable slices in small batches doing the beetroot slices separately – once cooked the beetroot ones can be mixed with the others. Fry until crisp. Drain well and sprinkle with salt. Reheat briefly by spreading out in a roasting tin and placing in a very hot oven for a couple of minutes.

Sautéed Savoy

1 small savoy cabbage
2 cloves oak-smoked garlic
1 tbs olive oil

Shred the savoy and crush the garlic. Mix the two together with the oil in a heavy-based pan. Place over a low heat, covered, for 10 minutes, shaking occasionally. Serve.

Pastiche Gascon

125 g/4 oz pruneaux d'Agen
150 ml/5 fl oz Armagnac
125 g/4 oz unsalted butter
8 filo pastry sheets
90 g/3 oz sugar
450 g/1 lb Cox's or Reinette apples
60 g/2 oz shelled walnuts
double cream to serve

Soak the chopped, stoned prunes in the Armagnac for at least 2 hours but preferably overnight.

Melt the butter. Grease a deep loose-bottomed 20 cm/8 in flan tin. Lay one sheet of filo into it, draping it over the sides. Brush it with butter, sprinkle it lightly with sugar then place another sheet of filo over it, at 45° to the first. Repeat the process 5 times. Peel and slice the apples and pile them over the base of the pastry. Top with the walnuts and then the prunes with any remaining Armagnac (if they have absorbed it all add a little extra).

Fold the filo edges in to make a patchwork top. Brush with the butter. Brush another sheet with butter, fold it in half and carefully pleat it like a fan. Lay it on the top covering half the pie. Repeat with the last sheet to cover the other half. Drizzle over any remaining butter and sprinkle with sugar. Bake at 200°C/400°F/gas mark 6 for about 30 minutes until crisp and golden. Serve warm with double cream.

Index